A County Wexford Family in the Land War

Maynooth Studies in Local History

SERIES EDITOR   Raymond Gillespie

This is one of six titles to be published in the Maynooth Studies in Local History series in 2002. The first forty titles were published by Irish Academic Press; the next volumes in the series are being published by Four Courts Press. The publication of this series is a reflection of the continued growth of interest in local and regional history within Ireland in recent years. That interest has manifested itself in diverse ways, including new research about the problems of local and regional societies in the past. These short books seek to make a contribution to that research. As in previous years most are drawn from theses completed as part of the MA in local history at NUI Maynooth.

The new studies published this year are concerned, as their predecessors have been, with the problem of how groups of people within relatively well-defined geographical contexts tried to resolve the problems presented by daily life in the past. Sometimes the areas studied may correspond to administrative units, sometimes not. One local society dealt with this year, Rossin, was an 'unofficial place', known as a distinct community only by those who lived there rather than by administrators. Even such unofficial places had problems in daily life. In some cases those problems had dramatic outcomes. Family jealousies over land and marriage could lead to murder. Elsewhere family networks shaped political actions during the land war. Although local historians are fascinated by the unusual and the violent the daily activities of ordinary life are equally important. The commonplace routines of making a living in an industrial town, worshipping at the local holy well in the way determined by local custom or in the parish church surrounded by one's neighbours are part of the story of the evolution of local societies and all are dealt with in this group of studies.

Taken together these new titles demonstrate yet again, if demonstration is still required, the vibrancy and diversity of the local societies which make up Ireland's past. In presenting this diversity to the modern world they also reveal the challenges which await other local historians to take up the stories of their own areas. In doing so they contribute to the lively discipline that local history has become in recent years.

Maynooth Studies in Local History: Number 41

A County Wexford Family in the Land War

The O'Hanlon Walshs of Knocktartan

Margaret Urwin

FOUR COURTS PRESS

Set in 10pt on 12pt Bembo by
Carrigboy Typesetting Services, County Cork for
FOUR COURTS PRESS LTD
Fumbally Lane, Dublin 8, Ireland
e-mail: info@four-courts-press.ie
http://www.four-courts-press.ie
and in North America for
FOUR COURTS PRESS
c/o ISBS, 5824 N.E. Hassalo Street, Portland, OR 97213.

ISBN 1–85182–709–9

Printed in Ireland by
ColourBooks Ltd, Dublin

Contents

Acknowledgements

I wish to acknowledge my indebtedness to the following for their assistance and co-operation in the course of my research for this study: the teaching staff of the Department of Modern History, NUI Maynooth, in particular Dr Raymond Gillespie and Professor R.V. Comerford; also the staff of the following repositories: the Russell Library, Maynooth College; the National Archives of Ireland; the National Library of Ireland; Department of Folklore, UCD; and the Valuation Office.

I wish to extend particular thanks to my friend Mary O'Loughlin for her invaluable assistance on Hook (Templetown) parish; Mr Tom Hickey, Ramstown, Fethard-on-Sea, Co. Wexford; Mr Richard Roche; my classmate, Susan Durack; the Revd Denis Kelly CC, Kiltealy, Co. Wexford; and Ms Sylvia O'Connor of M.J. O'Connor & Company, Solicitors, Wexford.

I am especially grateful to my husband, Mark, for his support and encouragement.

Introduction

In the nineteenth century the parish of Bannow encompassed the civil parishes of Ambrosetown, Ballingly, Ballymitty, Bannow and Kilcavan. This south Co. Wexford parish was located mainly in the barony of Bargy but partly in the barony of Shelmalier West. The townland of Knocktartan was located in the latter barony, on its northern boundary, adjoining the parish of Taghmon. The southern boundary of the parish forms a substantial part of the south Wexford coastline while its southwestern boundary lies on the shores of Bannow Bay.

The parish ensured a place in history when the Normans first set foot on Irish soil on Bannow Island in May 1169 and the area that became the baronies of Forth and Bargy evolved into their first colony. Having gained possession of the land of Bannow in the late twelfth century, they continued to hold it almost unchanged for 400 years. However, after the Rebellion of 1641, all the landlords of the parish, without exception, lost their lands, which were subsequently planted with Cromwellian soldiers.[1]

Thomas Boyse was the largest landlord in the parish in the second half of the nineteenth century. His ancestor, Nathaniel, had been granted the lands by Cromwell. An examination of Griffith's valuation of 1853 suggests that he owned approximately 4,500 acres, a third of the total acreage of the parish. The remaining two-thirds was owned by several landlords: the Revd Richard King and Arthur Annesley (Viscount Valentia) held nearly 1,500 acres each; Hamilton Knox Grogan Morgan of Johnstown Castle, near Wexford town, owned 1,300 acres while Thomas Martin held over 700 acres. The townland of Maudlintown, comprising 258 acres, was part of the Leigh estate, Rosegarland, in the adjoining parish of Clongeen. The Leigh family still holds a somewhat reduced Rosegarland today. A number of landlords owned a couple of hundred acres each, one of whom was Col. Charles Tottenham of Ballycurry, Ashford, Co. Wicklow. He held one townland in the parish – Knocktartan – comprising 196 statute acres, as well as much of the adjoining parish of Taghmon. He owned land all over counties Wexford and Wicklow and numbered among his tenants the Kennedys of Dunganstown.

The population of the parish declined fairly drastically between the Famine and the land war. It was reduced from 4,450 at its peak in 1841 to 2,770 in 1881, a loss of 37.8 per cent.

A thorough examination of the valuation books of 1853 for the parish has yielded the result contained in table 1, in terms of size of farm holdings. There is an absence of very large farms – even the home-farm of the Boyse estate contained just 259 acres.

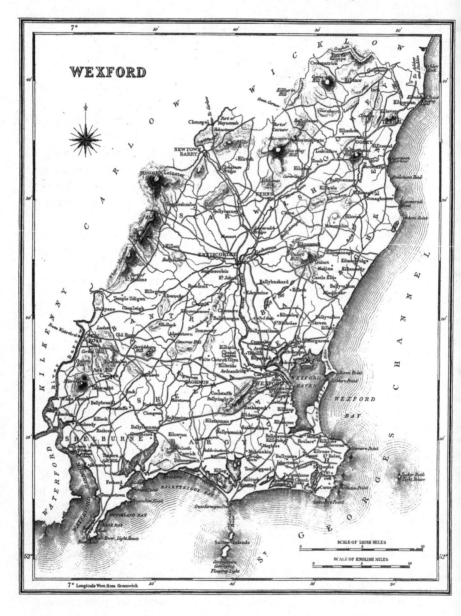

1 Map of Wexford, from Lewis, *Topographical dictionary*.

Table 1. Size of farm holdings, Bannow parish

Acreage	Number of holdings	Percentage of total
201–310	4	1.2
101–200	21	6.3
81–100	15	4.5
61–80	31	9.2
41–60	36	10.7
21–40	78	23.2
11–20	80	23.8
05–10	71	21.1
	336	

Source: Griffith's Valuation of Tenements, Co. Wexford (1853)

A further 307 householders, or 47.8 per cent, not included above, held less than five acres. This is almost half of the total householders (643). Inevitably, in a community that was almost exclusively agricultural, the great majority of these would be labourers. A small number would have other sources of income, for example, teachers, masons and blacksmiths. Of the 307 households of less than five acres, 78, or a quarter of them, were located in the villages of Tullycanna and Carrig.

Jones Hughes identifies the rural poor as those whose land was valued at less than £5. He states that, in the mid-nineteenth century in Co. Wexford, they were to be found in 'hamlets of labourers that never acquire institutions or administrative functions'. From Bannow parish he chooses Tullycanna as an example.[2] He also asserts that the poor were also to be found in what came to be known as chapel villages. In Tullycanna 85 per cent of the households fall into the poor category as defined by Jones Hughes while in Carrig (a chapel village) 74 per cent did so. The population of these two villages shows a drastic reduction between the Famine (1851 Census) and the beginning of the land war (1881 Census), particularly that of Tullycanna which decreased from 341 persons in 1851 to 129 in 1881, a shocking 62.2 per cent fall. Carrig's population shrunk from 342 inhabitants in 1851 to 184 in 1881, a fall of 46.2 per cent. The decline in these two villages compares very unfavourably with the overall parish decrease of 37.8 per cent. This is surely an important indicator that the great majority of those who emigrated were landless labourers.

1. Family background and the beginning of the O'Hanlon Walshs' involvement in land agitation

The children of the Walsh, or O'Hanlon Walsh, family of Knocktartan, who were born in the 1840s, are the subjects of this work. They grew to adulthood in a period of considerable change in their community. Their own townland of Knocktartan suffered no decrease in its population before the 1860s. According to Griffith's valuation, it comprised four households in October 1852.[1] The acreage was 196 statute acres or 120 Irish acres, which was divided between the four tenant farmers – the Walsh family holding 67 statute acres, the Doran family 65, the Ennis family 34 and 30 acres were held by the McGrath family. From 1852 to 1881 these four families held these farms, the only change being a passing on to the next generation. No labourers occupied a house on the townland throughout this period.

The Walshs and the Ennises were cousins, John Walsh's mother being Mary Anne Ennis. At least four surviving children, two sons, Nicholas and David and two daughters, Mary Anne and Margaret, were born to John and Mary Walsh, formerly O'Hanlon, during the 1840s – Nicholas c.1842–3,[2] David 1844;[3] Mary Anne either 1845[4] or possibly 1851[5] and Margaret 1849.[6] By October 1852, when Griffith's surveyor carried out the valuation of their townland, John Walsh was dead and his widow, Mary, was the tenant. Their land and buildings were valued at £32.10s. 6d. while the annual rent was £40.18s. 5d., 26 per cent above valuation. All the rents on the townland were above valuation – McGraths' by only 5.5 per cent; Ennises' by 29 per cent and Dorans' by a staggering 35.5 per cent. Despite the apparent inequalities in the rents charged on the townland, only the Walshs became actively involved in Land League agitation. The leases on the farms had all expired in 1848.[7] The Walshs were in the top 20 per cent in the parish in terms of farm size, one of only 71 holdings that exceeded 60 acres.

David (and probably Nicholas) Walsh, were lucky enough to receive a secondary education at St Peter's College, Wexford. In 1867, David, who may have been already studying for the priesthood at the time, responded to a notice in his local newspaper advertising the vacancy of a bourse of the Roche Foundation at the University of Louvain, Belgium. In a letter to Dr Russell, Maynooth College, dated 8 April 1868, Dublin Castle informed him that the three students recommended by Her Majesty's Government for three

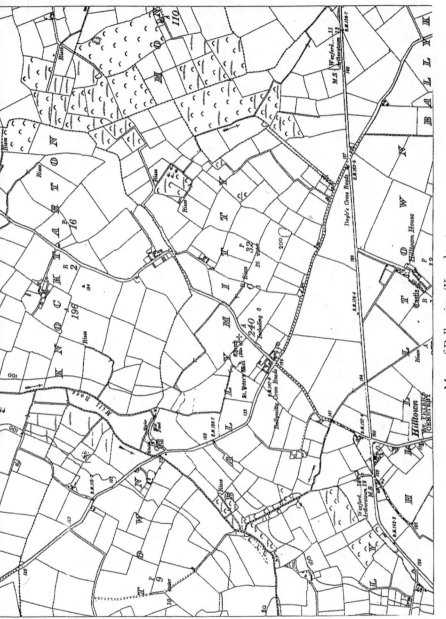

2 Map of Ballymitty/Knocktartan.

vacant bourses had been accepted and appointed by the Belgian Provincial Commission. Enclosed with the letter was a communication received from Howard de Walden of the British Embassy in Brussels, dated 31 March 1868, in which the three students were named as Owens, Mulryan and Walsh.[8] However, it would appear that David Walsh had already been a student at Louvain from 1867. He was listed as a recipient of 600 francs from the Roche Foundation in the years 1867–8 and again in 1868–9. It seems likely that David Walsh completed a further two years' study at Louvain, as his ordination did not take place until 1 November 1871 at the Convent of Mercy, Enniscorthy, Co. Wexford.[9]

In a pamphlet printed by order of the British Embassy *c.*1807, the Roche Foundation was stated to be specifically established for the study of rhetoric, philosophy and theology.[10] It was established by the Revd David Roche, parish priest of Wexford from 1686 to 1724, and was formally made over to Louvain by his nephew, the Revd Paul Roche, PP of Wexford, in 1727. The first preference was to be given to the founder's next of kin, secondly to prospective students of the barony of Forth and thirdly of the diocese of Ferns. David Walsh likely came under the third category. The total capital amount of the foundation was £350 Irish. Both Frs David and Paul Roche were distinguished graduates of the University of Louvain.[11]

Despite the early death of John Walsh, these years of the late 1860s and early 1870s would seem to have been bright ones for Mary Walsh and her children. David was studying for the priesthood at Louvain and Margaret made, what her mother would likely have regarded as a very suitable marriage, with a substantial farmer from Cushenstown, near New Ross, who was 12 years her senior. She married Patrick O'Byrne *c.*1869 at the age of about 20. In 1901 the O'Byrne family were occupying a farmhouse containing 10 rooms and with seven windows at its front.[12] The two first-born sons of Patrick O'Byrne and Margaret Walsh would go on to be clergymen like their uncle, David. Their eldest, James, who was born in 1870, ultimately became parish priest of Kilmore on the south Wexford coast, while the second son, Maurice, served as a priest in South Africa.[13] Their third son, John, eventually inherited the family farm and served as a member of Wexford Co. Council,[14] while Patrick, the fourth son, inherited the Walsh family farm at Knocktartan in 1920.[15]

In 1870, Mary Walsh's elder son, Nicholas, was about 28 years old and was most likely running the farm, while Mary Anne also lived at home and did not marry until *c.*1900. David, following his ordination in November 1871, was appointed to the curacy of Caim, near Enniscorthy and subsequently served in Tinahely and Kilrane, near Rosslare, before being appointed to the Hook parish in March 1881.[16]

In April 1879 Michael Davitt founded the Land League at Irishtown, Co. Mayo. In October of that year, he and a number of colleagues organized a meeting in Dublin of tenant representatives from all over Ireland and the Irish National Land League was founded with Charles Stewart Parnell as president. The two main objectives of the League were to protect tenants from rack-renting and to achieve the eventual introduction of tenant ownership. The Land League was slow to get off the ground in Co. Wexford and in the southeast of Ireland generally. However, a public meeting held at New Ross on 26 September 1880, attended by Charles Stewart Parnell, began to set wheels in motion. Among the gathering at that first meeting were a number of strong tenant farmers from the parish of Bannow. Fr David Walsh of Knocktartan, then a curate in Kilrane, who was to become one of the most prominent figures in the land war in Co. Wexford, was also present. After the New Ross meeting, branches of the Land League began to be established all over the county. When Fr Walsh set up a branch in his parish, he changed the name of the townland in which the first meeting took place to Parnellstown, a name it retains to this day and declared his presbytery to be 3, Obstruction Row.[17] Thus, from the very beginning, Fr Davy, as he came to be known, was making his mark in a very imaginative way.

On 24 October 1880, Canon Tom Doyle, parish priest of Ramsgrange, organized a public meeting at Wellington Bridge in the parish of Bannow. This village was in a central position in south Co. Wexford, located on the main road between Wexford and Duncannon. The formidable Canon Doyle was a native of Tombrick, near Bunclody (Newtownbarry) whose mother had been a cousin of John Kelly of Killanne hanged on Wexford Bridge in 1798.[18] He was to be at the forefront of the land agitation for many years. He later opposed Fr Davy and considerable tensions arose between them.

The crowd who attended the meeting at Wellington Bridge was estimated by the reporter of the *Wexford People* as being 10,000 strong. Of course this newspaper was nationalist in its outlook and its editor, Edward Walsh, a staunch supporter of the Land League. The paper might have exaggerated the numbers at such meetings but, on the other hand, meetings were a novelty in rural areas and could be expected to have strong entertainment, as well as political, value. From the descriptions that survive, they would appear to have been, without exception, very colourful spectacles. In any event, the gathering included farmers, labourers, shopkeepers and tradesmen. Many women were present and it is salutary to note that some of them were actually on the platform, which was decorated with flags and banners. Fr Davy was there, along with a contingent from Parnellstown, as was his brother, Nicholas. The clergy were well to the fore, comprising five of the 11 speakers, including Fr Davy. Five resolutions were passed: resolving to replace landlordism with peasant proprietary; declaring confidence in Parnell; resolving to establish branches of the Land League; never to pay an unjust rent or to take the land of an evicted farm; to provide comfortable dwellings with plots of land for labourers of which they could become proprietors and never to desist from agitation until an Irish parliament was restored to College Green. Fr Davy, who seconded one of the motions, already appears to have gained considerable popularity, as he was cheered loudly throughout his speech. He asked his audience to 'stand unitedly together and to stick to Mr Parnell and the Land League'.[19] In the weeks that followed the Wellington Bridge meeting, and another meeting at Gorey at which Fr Davy was again a speaker, the establishment of Land League branches was accelerated throughout the county and in early December 1880 one was set up in Bannow.

In November 1880, the Co. Wexford tenants of Col. Charles Tottenham of Ballycurry, Ashford, Co. Wicklow, got together and agreed that Griffith's valuation was sufficient rent to offer. The tenants were scattered around the county in isolated groups from Mountgarrett, near New Ross, to Ballymitty (Knocktartan). Sixty tenants were present, representing the townlands of Ballykerogue, Dunganstown, Ballintubber, Lacken, Ryleen, Knocktartan, Redhouse and Mount Elliott.[20] After their first meeting a memorial was forwarded to Col. Tottenham, advising him of their decision. Tottenham's agent, Thomas Boyd, attended their second meeting and read to them Tottenham's reply. This was an absolute rejection of their offer but he agreed to a reduction of 10 per cent if the rent was paid within an 'immediate and specified' date. The tenants refused this offer.[21] Proceedings were begun against the tenants in January 1881. In February, John Meehan of Redhouse, who held two farms from Tottenham, one on which he resided and another outfarm of marshland by the river Barrow, was served with a notice to quit. The rent being demanded for the outfarm was £81 while the valuation was only £43. Meehan gave up possession of his outfarm but compromised by paying the rent on his homefarm.[22]

On 16 February, at a special meeting of Carrig-on-Bannow Land League, called because of writs having been served on the tenants of Jones King, Bannow, attorney's letters on Tottenham's tenants in Knocktartan and also on the tenants of Boxwell in the parish. It was resolved that the branch would bear any legal costs in these cases. Nicholas Walsh was the only tenant from Knocktartan present at the meeting.[23] On 4 March, the tenants' interest in the lands of Ballintubber, Rathgerogue, Ryleen and Mount Elliot was sold in Wexford county courthouse.[24] The situation of the Tottenham tenantry was again the most important agenda item for New Ross Land League when it met on 9 March. Nicholas Walsh and several other Tottenham tenants were in attendance, as well as his brother-in-law, Patrick O'Byrne of Cushenstown. The League resolved to pay their legal expenses and to bring their case before the central League, asking for their assistance.[25] On 25 March, the first eviction on the Tottenham estate took place at Dunganstown. The farm was rented by Patrick Hunt, a New Ross businessman, but was sub-let to a man named John Molloy. Hunt claimed to have spent £200 on the farm of 30 statute acres for which he had seen no return. Molloy was ejected, his furniture removed and his livestock turned onto the road.[26] On 29 March, it was remarked at a meeting of New Ross Land League that it was pointless for the Tottenham tenantry to wait for the landlord to heap on legal costs and then pay in full. If they were not going to resist they might as well pay before writs were served on them. It was also remarked that Tottenham was the worst landlord and Boyd the worst agent in the district. On 31 March, four tenants in Ballintubber paid their rents in full, plus costs, under threat of immediate eviction. Two tenants in Lacken and one in Ryleen paid a portion of the rent due and agreed to pay the remainder after the next fair of New Ross.[27] By 14 April, it would appear that the Tottenham tenants on Knocktartan townland, with the exception of the Walshs, had paid their rent 'behind the backs of their fellow tenants' as a vote of censure was passed against them at a meeting of Carrig-on-Bannow League.[28]

Tottenham's agent, Thomas Boyd (whose brother was Dr James Boyd of Kiltra, in Bannow parish, the local dispensary doctor) was himself a fairly substantial landlord, owning 470 acres in Co. Wexford, including the townlands of Harristown Reask in Bannow/Kilcavan parish. He also owned 985 acres in Co. Kilkenny where he lived close to New Ross, at Chilcomb Lodge.[29] He had a solicitor's practice in New Ross and was crown prosecutor for Co. Tipperary. Throughout the 1880s his clients were invariably landlords whom he represented against their tenants. Agents were often local solicitors, retired army officers or wealthy gentlemen.[30]

The only townland owned by Tottenham in Bannow/Ballymitty was Knocktartan. He owned a substantial part of the adjoining parish of Taghmon out of a total of 7,066 acres in Co. Wexford.[31] As previously noted, the Walsh family, along with two of the three other tenants on the townland, had been paying well above Griffith's valuation since at least 1852. Mary Walsh's rent was reported to have been increased by 5s. per acre on the death of her husband.[32] As we saw, this occurred prior to October 1852. Therefore, if the newspaper report is correct, Mary Walsh's rent had not been raised in 30 years but, on the other hand, it was 26 per cent higher than the valuation for all of this period. Terence Dooley argues that by the late 1870s, Griffith's valuation, which had been based on 1849–51 prices, was perhaps as much as 33 per cent below the real letting value of land.[33] However, it would appear that Mary Walsh had been paying Tottenham 26 per cent above the valuation since 1852 or perhaps earlier, depending on when exactly her husband died.

From the viewpoint of tenant farmers, Thomas Boyd would become a notorious figure in the county over the coming decade. Boyd's younger son was murdered near their home in August 1880, three months prior to the Tottenham tenant meetings. His murder was classified by the authorities as an agrarian outrage. On 8 August 1880, while travelling on a side-car from their residence to their farm, Thomas Boyd, his two sons, Evans and Charles, and nephew, Gladwell, were ambushed at Shanbogh on the new road from New Ross to Waterford by three armed and masked assailants, who were each said to have fired at the car almost simultaneously. The intention was, presumably, to kill Boyd and his two sons. However, Evans was only slightly wounded, while the nephew, Gladwell, escaped uninjured. Thomas received a wound to the shoulder, which was not serious but Charles, not yet 21 years old, and a law student at Trinity College, Dublin, was not so lucky. He was shot in the left side, just below the heart, and died the following day despite having been attended to by his two uncles, Dr John Boyd, New Ross and Dr James Boyd, Kiltra, Bannow. Evans had driven out to Kiltra soon after the shooting to collect his Uncle James and cousin, Bagenal.[34]

The police later found cartridges at the scene, which they claimed, belonged to the rifles supplied to the army and constabulary by the government. The rifles used were subsequently found and were said to be Enfield military rifles of the 1871 design, with bayonets attached. This murder occurred before the establishment of the Land League in either Kilkenny or Wexford and was, therefore, unconnected with Land League activity.

Several members of the extended Phelan family, including two brothers, Walter and John were arrested immediately after the shooting. Most of them, including their sister, Anastasia, were eventually released, but Walter and John were charged with murder. The Phelans were tenants of Thomas Boyd and a possible motive for their alleged involvement was offered in the return of outrages for 1880. When Boyd bought the townland of Shanbogh from the landed estates court in 1872 there were about thirty tenants resident on the property. He had the property revaluated and an increase in rent followed. All the tenants agreed to the increase with the exception of Richard Phelan, James Phelan and two other tenants. After this, Boyd always demanded that the Phelans pay their rent on the due date while imposing no such punctuality on his other tenants. In the spring of 1880, he gave seed and lime to all his tenants, with the exception of the Phelans.[35]

The case against John and Walter Phelan was adjourned at Waterford winter assizes and again at Kilkenny spring assizes on 14 March 1881.[36] It was eventually heard at queen's bench on 27 June 1881 but only Walter Phelan stood trial. At the end of four days the Dublin jury acquitted him, the only evidence against him being that of Evans Boyd who claimed to have noticed a similarity of voice, height and gait between one of the assailants and Walter Phelan. One would expect that the murder of his son, Charles, and the acquittal of Walter Phelan could have contributed to Thomas Boyd's attitude towards Land League agitation. On 23 March, he had actually served the brother and uncle of the Phelan brothers with a formal notice to quit their tenant farms by 29 September although both tenants had paid their rents in full.[37]

Co-incidentally, on the very day that Walter Phelan was acquitted, 30 June 1881, the Walsh family, having refused to pay their rent, was evicted from their farm in Knocktartan. Neither the landlord, Tottenham, nor his agent, Boyd, was present. Mary Walsh offered what she considered to be a fair rent, but this was refused. Eighty policemen from Enniscorthy and Wexford were in attendance. The sheriff and bailiff proceeded with the eviction. The house was unoccupied and the furniture was flung onto the road. It was a day of torrential rain and there was difficulty in removing the cattle and horses from off the land. Fr Walsh, who had been transferred from Kilrane to Hook (Templetown) parish on 23 March 1881, arrived at the scene with a contingent from his new parish. He, too, was said to have offered what he considered to be a fair rent but, again, this was refused.[38] This eviction was the first to occur in the parish in these early days of the land agitation. The Walsh family allowed themselves to be evicted, not because they could not afford the rent, but because they had made a decision to stand by the principles of the Land League, by the resolution made at Wellington Bridge not to pay what they considered to be an unjust rent and by the decision made at New Ross by the tenants of Col. Tottenham. Their act of defiance, and indeed sacrifice, does not appear to have been emulated by the other tenants, despite their pledge.

A huge Land League meeting was planned for the village of Taghmon for the feast of the Assumption, 15 August 1881. On 9 August, in anticipation of the meeting, Sub-Inspector Townley Ball of Taghmon wrote to the inspector general in Dublin Castle submitting a poster advertising the meeting and a list of resolutions to be proposed. He requested an extra force of at least 25 policemen 'to keep the peace' as he expected large crowds due to the meeting being held on 'Lady Day'.[39]

On the day itself local women ensured that the village was beautifully decorated with triumphal arches, flags and banners. The Revd Davy Walsh made a flamboyant entrance into the village on horseback, leading about two hundred men from the Hook. His colourful actions suggest he saw himself as a leader and not just a curate in a quiet backwater, and that he was developing his public persona very carefully. Prior to his triumphant entry into Taghmon he and the Hook contingent had met with members of the Carrig-on-Bannow League, including his brother, Nicholas, at the evicted family home in Knocktartan, three miles from Taghmon. Since the eviction, the Walsh family had continued to occupy one of the barns on the property. They claimed that because the sheriff had failed to drive a 'spirited' mare off the land on the day of the eviction, possession had not been secured by the landlord, with the exception of the dwelling house, now being guarded by 'emergencymen'. So-called emergencymen were used by the sheriff to assist at evictions and to guard evicted properties. They were brought in from another area and were never locals.

The Hook and Carrig-on-Bannow Leaguers surrounded the house, while Fr Davy knocked on the door demanding an item of furniture belonging to his mother, which he claimed, was still inside. When the door was eventually opened by an emergencyman, he was informed by Fr Davy that they would call again on their return from Taghmon. Before they travelled on together to the meeting, they proceeded to burn effigies of the emergencymen and bedecked the defiant mare in green and white ribbons. An arch, spanning the road, had previously been erected, displaying a photograph of Parnell and bearing the mottoes: 'Be true to the Land League' and 'Welcome to the Barn'. The emergencymen reported to Sub-Inspector Ball that Fr Davy had demanded admittance to the house and, when refused, had threatened to come back after the meeting was over. Ball had to reinforce the men at the 'Knocktartan Protection Post' and, at a late hour, telegraphed the county inspector, J.J. Jones, requesting an extra force.[40]

Fifteen thousand people had gathered in Taghmon, among them Patrick O'Byrne, Cushenstown, brother-in-law of the Walshs. His wife, Margaret, may also have been present because a Mrs O'Byrne is listed among those on the women's platform. Sub-Inspector Ball was already aware of the activities of Nicholas and Fr Davy Walsh at Knocktartan on their way to the meeting and, as soon as Fr Davy ascended the platform, asked to speak privately with him. The priest declined and asked the sub-inspector to state publicly what his business was but Ball refused to comply with his request.

Seventeen clergymen were on the platform, including Fr Davy. Land League branches from all over the county were well represented. The Land Bill going through parliament was condemned as being totally inadequate, the gains made so far by the Land League were recounted, there were demands that the government make provision for the labourers, and 'land-grabbers' were warned they would be boycotted. This was in accordance with the philosophy of the Land League which opposed violence and recommended, instead, that any man who took a farm from which another tenant had been evicted, should be shunned. Fr Davy was the final speaker and, on stepping forward, he received an enthusiastic ovation, which lasted several minutes. He spoke briefly and read an extract from an article that had been published in the *Daily Express*. The article related to the eviction of his family and claimed that his followers, who were referred to as the 'Hook 200' (a name which they adopted from that moment) were 'well-primed with whiskey'. This allegation was denied categorically by Fr Davy. He complimented the Carrig-on-Bannow branch and warned against labourers cutting hay on evicted farms.[41] A police sub-constable, Nicholas Mullan, was later to claim that Fr Davy had held up a placard at the Taghmon meeting describing himself as 'D. O'Hanlon Walsh, Head Organiser of the Co. Wexford'.[42] This claim is dubious because there is no evidence of either Fr Davy, or his brother, Nicholas, using the prefix 'O'Hanlon' at that time. At the end of December, when the authorities were seriously considering arresting Fr Davy under the Protection of Person and Property Act, a précis of his activities was prepared. This included the information that his speech at the Taghmon meeting had been 'most violent' and that he had made a serious 'hinting' allusion to the use of infernal machines (explosive devices).[43] If Fr Davy made such remarks the *People* newspaper did not report them, for obvious reasons.

In a letter to the editor of the same newspaper, published on 27 August, Fr Davy condemned the Land Commission, which, under the new Land Act, had been established in order to hold hearings and decide fair rents in disputed cases. He declared that he would take no part in it.

By late August, the Walsh family and their farm had become a *cause célèbre*. On 29 of that month, in a model example of social cohesion, help arrived at Knocktartan from all over the parish in order to harvest ten Irish acres of barley. Early that morning, about 50 vehicles left Carrig, each carrying between five and eight men. Leading the procession was a reaping machine manufactured by Pierces of Wexford and owned by Denis Crosbie of Bannow. Accompanied by the Bannow fife and drum band they arrived at Knocktartan at 11 o'clock. By noon, there were several reaping machines and binders waiting their turn. Among those in attendance was an old man of 85 on crutches, whose name was John Maloney. Wearing a Land League scarf, the Parnell medal and the green card of Bannow Land League, he was given the privilege of tying the first sheaf. Maloney's father had been involved in the rebellion of 1798 and John, in his mother's arms, had been present at the battle of Horetown, in the adjoining parish of Clongeen.[44] It was important, in Co. Wexford, to link the rebellion of 1798 with the Land League in order to affirm the legitimacy of the latter's cause and to reinforce the continuity of the people's struggle against oppression. A dozen local farmers, including Nicholas Walsh, had their reaping machines in use and the two fields of barley – Horse Park and White Meadow – were harvested and the last sheaf tied by 3.30 p.m. Fr Davy then spoke to his neighbours and friends. He chose his platform carefully – the ruins of an old cottage on the farm and made reference to the happy home the ruined cottage had once been. His use of the cottage ruins may have been intended as a powerful image suggesting the evicted family 'without a roof' whereas, of course, the farmhouse from which his family had been evicted was still perfectly intact, although occupied by emergencymen. During the course of his speech he made certain references to Taghmon shopkeepers – that some were genuine Land Leaguers while others were 'only playing a game'. In what may have been a reference to Mary Stafford, a Taghmon shopkeeper, who had inadvertently lent her car to the police on the day of the Knocktartan eviction, he said people were not obliged to give their cars or other goods to the police or emergencymen. He also seemed to suggest that some Taghmon shopkeepers were supplying emergencymen. He advised his audience to 'shun bad company'.[45]

A statement was published in the same edition of the *People*, announcing that, 'if members of Taghmon Land League and the people of Taghmon had known for sure that the Knocktartan harvest was to be saved, they would have been there to assist'. This would appear to indicate the existence of an undercurrent of tension, possibly between farmers and shopkeepers in the locality, despite the fact that, generally, farmers and shopkeepers had formed a new rural alliance at this time. This note of discord was very much at odds with the harmony of the farmers and labourers who saved the Knocktartan harvest.

Throughout this period the Walsh family continued to occupy a barn on the farm. Many years later, on the death of Nicholas, an unidentified friend commented in an obituary that this barn became 'the rendezvous of all agitators'. He said he had taken tea there in 1881 with such celebrities as Joe Biggar, Tim Healy and John Barry, all members of parliament. On 13 October, this occupancy resulted in Mrs Mary Walsh, her daughter Mary Anne and son Nicholas, together with the 'Land League Sergeant,' Michael O'Grady, and their servant, Patrick Lacy, being summoned at Taghmon petty sessions by Col. Tottenham for unlawful trespass on his property at Knocktartan. Michael O'Grady's job was to patrol and guard the farm for the Walsh family, keeping an eye on any neighbours who might be tempted to take the grass or interfere with the farm in any way. The case was heard amid great uproar with Fr Davy eventually restoring calm. It was dismissed as it was held that the defendants had a *bona fide* belief that they were in legal possession, the sheriff having failed to remove all the stock from the farm. The statement made by John Colfer, New Ross, solicitor for the Walsh family, provides details of the stock held on the farm on the day of the eviction. There were eight cows, one bull, five heifers, and three young horses, a sow and 14 pigs that were not removed. At the time a quarter of the farm was under barley. This, then, was a prosperous farm and this insight confirms that the Walsh family made a deliberate choice in allowing themselves to be evicted.

When they emerged from the courthouse, there was great excitement among the crowd gathered outside and Nicholas Wash was carried shoulder-high through the village, with the crowd cheering for the Land League and Parnell. Constable Allshire of Duncannon would later claim that the three men who carried Nicholas Walsh that day were from Hook and followers of Fr Davy. He further claimed that the 'yelling crowd' who followed them was mostly from the Hook estate.[46] This claim was a slight exaggeration, as it seems more than likely that members of Carrig-on-Bannow and Taghmon Land Leagues were present as well. Fr Davy addressed the assembled crowd from a window of Bartle Brennan's residence. He warned of tenants paying rents behind the backs of other tenants and openly named two alleged culprits – Rossiter and Moran – who may have been tenants of the Boyse estate in Bannow. He read aloud from a document, which he claimed was a letter from the Walshs' former landlord, Col. Tottenham, to his wine merchant in London. In the letter, Tottenham regretted he was unable to purchase his annual stock of 'Montillo' that year, because such a purchase would be inconvenient. Fr Davy declared that it would be inconvenient for much longer than a year because they were not going to pay 'unjust rackrents' so that the landlords might indulge in 'Montillo' at 24s. a bottle.[47]

As the year 1881 was drawing to a close, the Land League was firmly established throughout Co. Wexford with the lead being given by the clergy and the stronger tenant farmers. A glance through the names of those who were in attendance at the Taghmon meeting would suggest that few others were involved at leadership level. Certainly Edward Walsh, editor of the *People* newspaper was present, as well as members of Wexford Borough Home Rule Club and a number of shopkeepers. There were apologies from Dr Joseph Cardiff of Carrigbyrne and John Colfer, the New Ross solicitor who acted for the Walsh family. Because of the Land Bill proceeding through the house of commons, local MPs were unable to attend and they, too, sent apologies.

The Walsh family had, by that time, reached a position of prominence in local Land League activity. Fr Davy, in particular, had become incredibly popular with the people and was playing a starring role in the agitation. However, other Tottenham tenants had reneged on the agreement made at New Ross and, when faced with eviction, had capitulated.

2. The Revd David O'Hanlon Walsh and the tenants of the marquis of Ely

Fr Davy, as noted earlier, was appointed curate at the Hook (Templetown) parish in March 1881 and quickly gathered around him a strong following, as evidenced at the Walsh eviction in June, the Taghmon meeting in August and the court case at Taghmon petty sessions in October. The Hook is approximately 12 miles distant from Knocktartan. As soon as he established himself in the parish, he set about renaming buildings and streets as he had done in his previous posting. The Hook was one of the few rural parishes possessing a reading room and this was promptly renamed 6, Dillon Place by Fr Davy. Reading rooms provided ordinary people with access to local and national newspapers where the literate would read aloud to those who were illiterate. His presbytery was named Davitt Hall (fig. 3), while two rows of cottages in the village of Fethard-on-Sea were renamed Dynamite Row and Obstruction Place referring to tactics adopted by the nationalist movement in the 1880s.[1]

Fr David Walsh had begun to make a name for himself in his previous posting at Kilrane, near Rosslare. As well as renaming the townland in which that branch of the Land League was founded, he had also named his residence Parnell Cottage. He had agitated for Griffith's valuation to be accepted on the Edwards and Trimmer estates.[2] By his criticism of the excessive rents on the Trimmer estate he had incurred the wrath of its owner, John Greene, also proprietor of the *Wexford Independent*, regarded as an organ of the establishment. Fr Davy was condemned and his motives questioned in an editorial in that newspaper.[3]

However, his former parishioners in Kilrane held him in high regard. In May 1881 a deputation visited him in his new residence, Davitt Hall, where they presented him with a glowing address and a purse of gold, in recognition of the leadership he had given in the struggle against their landlords. Fr Davy was embarrassed by their magnanimous tribute having spent just thirteen months as their curate.[4]

On 29 September 1881, Fr. Davy organized a meeting of Ely's tenants at Poulfur, near Fethard-on-Sea. The Wexford seat of the marquis of Ely was at Loftus Hall on the Hook peninsula. Ely was an absentee landlord who lived at Dover in England. On 1 October, Sub-Inspector Townley Ball of Taghmon, the senior policeman for the whole area, forwarded a report of the meeting, which he had received from a local constable, to the inspector general of the RIC. Dr Joseph Cardiff, Carrigbyrne, had chaired the meeting. Resolutions

3 Davitt Hall, formerly Templetown parish presbytery and
once home of the Revd David O'Hanlon Walsh.

were allegedly passed that no rent at all would be paid until rack-rents were
abolished, or if Co. Wexford was proclaimed, or if any of those in attendance
were arrested. Fr Davy announced that he would appoint watchmen in each
townland to report to him if anyone attempted to pay rent. The aspect of the
meeting, which appeared to alarm the police, was Fr Davy's alleged threatening language. He referred to a certain Fr Doyle having once saved an agent's
life but declared he would not 'go between an agent or a landlord' to save
them. Ball expressed the view that Fr Davy was endeavouring to get himself
arrested or to get the county, or even his district, proclaimed, in order to
throw discredit on the Land Act.[5]

A few days later Fr Davy again allegedly used threatening language at a
meeting in the Reading Room. It was claimed that he declared: 'May the Lord
have mercy on the soul of the man who pays his rent.' Godfrey Taylor, agent of
the marquis of Ely, had informed Ball that two men had been instructed to
watch the estate office.[6] Fr Davy had the support of his parish priest for a
meeting on 9 October to establish a separate League branch for the parish of

Hook. Fr Richard Kelly was elected honorary treasurer. This meeting was adjourned and reconvened on 14 October. By this time C.S. Parnell, John Dillon and William O'Brien had been arrested. These arrests were denounced by Fr Davy. He told his audience that they must redouble their efforts and watch closely those whom they suspected of wavering. He condemned those traders of New Ross who were supplying goods to emergencymen. A resolution was passed to boycott hunting and all other sports and amusements supported by landlords or their associates. Nicholas Walsh was present at the meeting and was unanimously elected as an honorary member of the committee.[7]

At the next meeting held on 23 October, Constable Nicholas Mullan was there to provide a full account to his superior. Fr Davy repeated his story about a certain Fr Doyle having come to the aid of an agent named Hare. Mullan was probably too young to realise that Pat Hare had been the previous agent on the Ely estate and was an uncle of the present agent, Godfrey Taylor. Hare had carried out the evictions of 121 tenants on the estate in 1865. The Fr Doyle who had intervened to save Hare from being shot was, most probably, Canon Tom Doyle who had been appointed parish priest of nearby Ramsgrange in 1863.[8] Fr Davy allegedly stated that he wouldn't intercede to save an agent from a fate he might deserve. He named the New Ross traders who were supplying provisions to the emergencymen at Knocktartan. Mullan claimed that Fr Walsh held up a notice bearing the words: 'No Rent,' saying it had been signed by C.S. Parnell and A.J. Kettle in Kilmainham gaol, Michael Davitt in Portland prison and added that it was now signed by 'David O'Hanlon Walsh'.[9] The public display of this placard shows that Fr Davy had immediately endorsed the 'No rent manifesto' as issued from prison by the leaders of the Land League. This reference by Mullan to the use of the prefix 'O'Hanlon' is credible because Fr Davy used the full name 'O'Hanlon Walsh' for the first time in a letter written to the *People* newspaper, dated that very day. It was also very quickly adopted by his brother, Nicholas. The use of the double surname suggests that the family had a sense of their increasing status and influence among the people, not just in Hook and Bannow parishes, but also in several parts of south Wexford. The inclusion of their mother's surname, that of one of the foremost Ulster septs, may also have been an attempt to authenticate their old Irish roots.

The 'No Rent Manifesto' caused the government to declare the League illegal. On 20 October a proclamation was issued, prohibiting meetings being held under the title of 'Land League'. Fr Davy called an emergency meeting for Thursday, 27 October, to inform people that the meeting planned for the following Sunday could not go ahead under the usual title. Constable Edward Boland, Fethard, called on Fr Davy to disperse this emergency meeting who responded by asking, rhetorically, who was to advise the people if their priests could not guide them, especially if they should get wild ideas into their heads, such as seeking revenge. Fr Davy's brother, Nicholas and another prominent

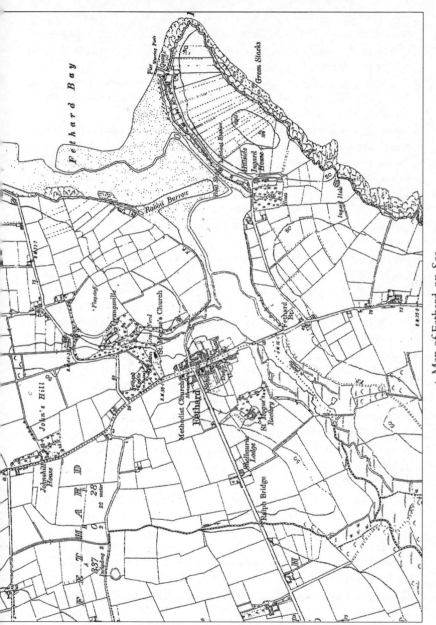

4 Map of Fethard-on-Sea.

Land Leaguer and strong farmer from Bannow were present. Constable Boland surmised that the reason for their attendance was to represent the Carrig-on-Bannow Land League, some of whose members were holding out against their landlord, Captain Boyse.

An episode occurred shortly afterwards that clearly shows the impetuous nature of Fr Davy and his predilection for the dramatic. His friend, Dr Joe Cardiff, was arrested on the morning of 28 October under the Protection of Person and Property (Ireland) Act 1881. This Act had been passed the previous March and gave powers, effectively, to intern suspects without trial. It allowed for the arrest and legal detention 'of any person suspected of an act of violence or intimidation, or the inciting to an act of violence or intimidation'.[10] It stipulated that 'any person detained under this Act shall be treated as a person accused of crime and not as a convicted prisoner.'[11]

On the afternoon of that day, 28 October, Fr Davy drove at speed into the town of New Ross in Dr Cardiff's croydon and wearing the doctor's coat and hat. He paid a visit to Ryan's public house as he usually did on visits to the town. On leaving, he was carried to his croydon by a large crowd. Constable Philip Palmer's report of the event seems to have blown it out of all proportion. He enclosed an article from the *Daily Express* with his report. The article claimed that Fr Davy had used violent language and that the local parish priest had to be sent for in order to prevent a riot. Palmer could not ascertain whether Fr Davy was drunk at the time nor could he give an accurate account as to his sanity. He claimed that locals had told him that the priest was viewed around Fethard as being mad and that 'he does be going around the strand there with a woman's hat on him'. He rather contradicted himself by adding that he was also informed that the priest wielded a great deal of influence among the farmers around Fethard.[12] When Palmer's superior, Sub-Inspector Wilson, returned from leave, he wrote to the authorities playing down Fr Davy's actions, suggesting he was eccentric. Under Secretary Burke decided that no proceedings should be taken against him.[13]

The first suggestion of the benefit that might be gained by Fr Davy's removal to another parish was made by Constable Benjamin Allshire when he stated that, if this happened, the tenants on the Ely estate would give up their agitation.[14] The local constables were, undoubtedly, the eyes and ears of Dublin Castle at parish and local level. Even the sermons preached in his church by Fr Davy were the subject of police reports. On 7 November, he allegedly told his congregation that if they broke their resolutions they should be shunned as they would a patient with smallpox. On 10 November, Ely's agent, Taylor, began corresponding with Chief Secretary Forster, alleging that many of his tenants would pay their rent but dare not, through fear of Fr Walsh and a few of his assistants.[15]

Police reports from mid-November 1881, reflect the expanding influence of Fr Davy with tenants on estates outside of Hook parish. This was a period of frenetic activity by him. On 12 November, he presided over a meeting of

5 The coach house at Davitt Hall.

6 Grangeville, formerly the home of Godfrey Lovelace Taylor,
agent to the marquis of Ely.

Clayton Brown's tenants at Scullabogue (Dr Joe Cardiff's area of influence) and insisted that they pay no rent until all political prisoners, including Dr Cardiff, were released. Also interned under the Protection Act was Pierce Meaney of St Leonard's in Tintern parish, adjoining the Hook. On the day following his trip to Scullabogue, Fr Davy, according to Sub-Inspector Ball, was 'scouring the countryside' seeking helpers to save crops and undertake farmwork on Meaney's farm. On 14 November, at the saving of the crops, he allegedly stated that, since the Land League had been declared illegal, more murders had been committed throughout the country than there had been for the previous two years. He predicted that there would be more murders in the coming months than there had been in the previous ten years. That same evening, he hosted a 'tea meeting' in Davitt Hall, his own home, where he made speeches to the women present and gave instructions for the boycotting of Andrew Barden, a strong tenant farmer on the Ely estate and a poor rate collector. Barden had 'broken the combination' by applying to the land court to fix his rent. Land courts had been established by the 1881 Land Act to enable tenants in dispute with their landlords to apply to the court for adjudication. Ball related that Fr Davy had given instructions that Barden should be ostracized – no one should sit near him at Mass or speak to him. If this is to be believed, the police must certainly have had an informant 'on the inside'. On the next day, 15 November, he was back in Tintern endeavouring to establish a Ladies' Land League and seeking funds for a 'Prisoners' Defence Fund'. On that same evening he travelled on to Newcastle, a townland in the parish of Clongeen, to urge people to gather in their hundreds at the forthcoming evictions on the Rosegarland estate of Francis Leigh fixed for 24 November.[16]

Fr Davy's energy and enthusiasm for the cause he had espoused seems quite remarkable, especially when one considers that the only modes of transport were either by horse and croydon, or side-car, or on horseback. These trips, on cold and probably often wet, winter days, must have been very difficult and not for the faint-hearted or the weak. Ball recognized this and commented to the inspector general of his 'ceaseless energy and persistence'. Interestingly, for whatever reason, Fr Davy does not appear to have concerned himself with the tenants on the Boyse estate in his native parish of Bannow, who were holding out against their landlord during that period.

The police became alarmed that crowds might gather on the Leigh estate, at Fr Davy's prompting, during the planned evictions. After communications between Ball, the resident magistrate and the county inspector, J.J. Jones, the inspector general issued a proclamation signed by the attorney general, prohibiting crowds from assembling at the scene of the evictions. Ball also requested that a RM, two sub-inspectors and a hundred policemen be present on the day. The local police began focusing on the personalities of some of Fr Davy's followers. Constable Allshire reported that two of them, Grace and Egan, were 'idle' while Shea and Hayes were men with 'nothing to lose and everything to gain'. He suggests that none of his followers was influential with the farmers, except for David Gleeson, a relative of Fr Davy's, 'who is a different class of a man, one who wouldn't commit an outrage' yet he believed there was no more zealous person in the cause. At the end of the month, Constable Philip Palmer wrote to the county inspector insisting that Fr Davy was leading a system of intimidation and called for his arrest under the Protection Act.[17]

Fr Davy's next act was to arrange for the sale of crops and stock of twenty-four farmers on the Ely estate who had been issued with writs by the marquis. He was enabled to do this through the assistance of his brother, Nicholas, who had acquired an auctioneer's licence. On 3 December, the county inspector informed the inspector general of this latest development, which would ensure that when the sheriff arrived, there would be nothing for him to seize. Notices of the forthcoming auction had been posted in Taghmon district. Following the auction the agent, Godfrey Taylor, wrote to the chief secretary claiming that Fr Davy and his brother, with a band and a 'large mob' carrying Land League banners, had gone from house to house selling the crops and stock. Fr Davy, in his usual fashion, rode on horseback at their head.[18]

The authorities were obviously becoming seriously alarmed by Fr Davy's activities. On 5 December, Robert Kennedy, RM for Wexford, suggested to the inspector general that the crown solicitor should visit Wexford and carry out an inquiry into his conduct. By this time he had established a branch of the Ladies' Land League in the Hook and a very busy Constable Boland reported on a meeting of theirs held at Templetown on 12 December. According to him, the meeting continued from 11 a.m. to 4 p.m. On Fr Davy's arrival, Boland enquired as to the object of the meeting stating that Bridget Connolly had informed him that she held the position of president. The priest allegedly replied that, for providing Boland with this information, she was now dismissed from her post. About 130 women and girls were present. In protest at the presence of the police, they sang songs about the Land League, land-grabbers and those interned in prison, popularly known as 'the suspects.' They sang 'The Wearing of the Green' and 'The Harp without the Crown,' all at the instigation of Fr Davy. He, himself, read a poem lamenting a young woman, Ellen McDonagh, who had recently been killed by a police bayonet at Belmullet, Co. Mayo. Boland claimed he felt threatened by a remark of Fr Davy's that neither of the two of them might be alive in six months' time. The women threw apples at the police, tried to press them out of the room and prevented them from taking notes. This gives us a powerful insight into the role played by women in the land agitation at this crucial time when the Land League was a banned organization. Fr Davy appears to have been the only male in the room, apart from the police. If Boland's report can be believed, he certainly was leading the women and sounded more than a little peremptory in his remark about Bridget Connolly, if one can take it seriously. The women of Hook parish were obviously very politically involved and could use their own initiative. It

7 Loftus Hall gatelodge.

is interesting to note that they had the freedom to spend most of Sunday at a meeting.

On that dark winter's evening, four large panes of glass in the windows of Loftus Hall gatelodge were smashed with stones. Loftus Hall was the newly built seat in Co. Wexford of the marquis of Ely. Ball sent details to County Inspector Jones categorizing the attack as an agrarian outrage – malicious injury to property. Ball claimed he had been unable to procure a car in Fethard to go to the scene, as nobody would give him one.[19]

On 17 December, Ball again wrote to Jones, this time expressing a wish to see Fr Davy prosecuted. His remarks that the priest's speeches were addressed to 'excited masses of half-wild but cunning, quick-witted peasants' suggest overtones of an imperialistic mindset. He claimed that Fr Davy had been involved in the most direct incitement to murder, which had already endangered Taylor's life and any tenant known to have paid his rent. Jones became alarmed on receipt of this letter and strongly recommended to the inspector general that extra troops should be stationed at nearby Duncannon Fort to be accompanied by an ambulance and wagons and horses because of the unavailability of transport.

As previously noted, Robert Kennedy RM had recommended that the crown solicitor should carry out an inquiry into Fr Davy's activities. This recommendation was acted on promptly and came to fruition rapidly as the inquiry was undertaken and the report furnished by 22 December. It appears to have been an entirely one-sided affair with eight policemen and the agent, Taylor, being the only people interviewed. No consideration seems to have been given to hearing from Fr Davy himself or any of the tenants on the estate. The first statement was that of Taylor and, as might be expected, he called for Fr Davy's removal. He claimed the priest had succeeded in influencing the entire south of Wexford 'from Hook to Kilmore coastways, around by New Ross and back to Hook'. He called for 100 to 200 troops to be stationed at Duncannon Fort and also for nightly patrols of military through the district, a move that could be expected, if carried out, to be highly unpopular. Taylor claimed that all placards were disseminated, through the Ladies' Land League, by Fr Davy. Sub-Inspector Wilson stated that the priest exerted considerable influence over Lord Templemore's estate at nearby Dunbrody and Clayton Brown's at Carrigbyrne. His view was that Fr Davy should be arrested and he claimed that respectable people in the district wanted him removed. Constable Edward Boland of Fethard, the man on the spot, stated that prior to Fr Davy's appointment to the Hook, only nine short months' previously, the district had been peaceful. He continued by giving an account of all the meetings presided over by the priest in the previous months and the statements made by him. He claimed that Fr Davy had threatened him by saying: 'You are a married man, perhaps before Christmas your wife may want the assistance of her neighbours.' He said the Ladies' Land League was just a cover name, presumably, for Land League activity. However, Boland was against his arrest in case he, himself, would suffer. He expected that he would be the one called upon to arrest Fr Davy and feared being labelled a 'priest hunter' and having to give evidence against him. Sub-Constable Cash referred to the priest making an example of Patrick Codd. The *People* had published a letter from Codd, of Littlegraigue in the parish of Bannow, the previous August. In it he complained that having inadvertently taken grass against the rules of Carrig-on-Bannow League, he had immediately given up the land as a result of their objection, at a serious financial loss to himself, but that this had not been enough to appease his neighbours.[20] It seems, from Cash's testimony, that Fr Davy had some involvement in this. Sub-Constable John Maher claimed that the priest had ordered people to buy only in shops where the Land League card was on display. He alleged he had private information that Fr Davy had threatened John Madden of Churchtown, who had paid his rent, by saying to him: 'It will be the last rent you will pay and may the Lord have mercy on your soul.' He further alleged that, at a private meeting, Ely tenants were asked to sign a paper binding them to pay no rent and to give up their land before doing so. He, too, claimed to be fearful of giving evidence against Fr Davy in case he would be shot but suggested that the priest and his followers should be removed. The final witness was Sub-Inspector Ball who also recommended the removal of Fr Davy and the arrest of his followers. His claim that the 'whole barony of Shelburne was in desolation and at the command of Fr Walsh' was obviously an exaggeration. His suggested method of dealing with the troublesome priest was to ensure that information should be sworn against him on the basis that statements he had made were incitement to murder rather than by summary arrest under the Protection Act. He proposed that the bishop should 'degrade' him and his followers should be arrested.

The crown solicitor conducting the inquiry concluded by describing Fr Davy as a 'pest' and noted the constables' fear of a public prosecution. The final sentence of his report reads as follows: 'If the bishop will not look at things as they are, then, in the absence of a prosecution, which does not seem advisable in my opinion, there is only one other course for the Government to take.'[21] Presumably, this 'one other course' meant arrest and internment under the Protection Act as, before the year was out, preparations were underway to do just that.

The local constables had reason to fear the consequences if they were ordered to arrest Fr Davy or, more particularly, if a prosecution was being sought, of giving evidence against him. However, Constable Maher's assertion that he was fearful of being shot seems a little overstated as no violence had been perpetrated in the locality with the single exception of the broken windows of Loftus Hall gatelodge. The only policeman who wanted a prosecution against Fr Davy was Ball, who did not live in the district. A memo on the state of Co. Wexford marked 'Confidential', dated 23 December, and written on the chief secretary's notepaper, noted that as many as 80 tenants were to be prosecuted on the Ely estate. The memo claimed that the worst part of the county was near Duncannon 'under the evil influence of Fr Walsh' and that by his speeches he had excited his 'wild followers' to commit outrages. There was a suggestion that the constabulary in the area should be strengthened.

By Christmas Day, Fr Davy was well aware that the bishop of Ferns had been informed of his activities. Boland alleged that in his Christmas Day sermon, he likened those who had reported him to the bishop to the Jews who, 'having first received Our Saviour, then turned around and crucified him'. He compared the government's actions with King Herod's putting to death of all children under the age of two, 'for law and order'. He told his congregation, as reported by Boland, that if he were removed from Templetown, they would know what to do. On 21 December the bishop had held an inquiry at New Ross into Fr Davy's conduct. This had resulted in his prohibition from preaching or being involved in politics in any way, on pain of being silenced.[22]

On 29 December, preparations began for the arrest of Fr Davy and eleven of his followers, under the Protection Act. The crimes listed for all twelve included an attack on the permanent post at Knocktartan on 15 August, preventing tenants from paying rent and attending the Land League auction. Fr Davy's list of crimes also included incitement to murder. These recommendations for arrests led to a high level meeting at Dublin Castle the following day, which was attended by Chief Secretary Forster; Under Secretary Burke; the solicitor general; Robert Kennedy RM, Wexford, and Sub-Inspector Ball,

Taghmon. The decision of the meeting was that no steps should be taken in relation to Fr Davy at that point, pending the result of further action on the part of the marquis of Ely for the recovery of rent. With regard to his followers, it was decided that there were insufficient grounds to bring them under the provision of the Protection Act. This was a complete climbdown, obviously decided at the highest level for pragmatic purposes. Being well aware of the far-reaching influence and popularity of Fr Davy they probably feared the consequences of such actions on tenants throughout south Co. Wexford. However, priests and leaders had been arrested in other parts of the country so they may have believed that the bishop's prohibition would have the desired effect with no necessity for them to take action. On 12 January 1882, Taylor alleged that Christmas dues of two of his tenants who had paid their rent had been returned to them in Templetown chapel and they were now actually prevented from even entering their place of worship. One of these was Andrew Barden, the poor rate collector. Taylor claimed that the bishop's reprimand had done little good.

Fr Davy's achievements in Hook parish and further afield over the previous nine months were quite phenomenal. He was utterly true to the principles of the Land League and was prepared to go to great lengths to ensure its success. He had organised the Ely tenants and instigated and developed their agitation against the absentee landlord, the marquis of Ely. In January 1882, a letter to the *People* declared the Hook to have been previously the most backward and most enslaved place in the country.[23] Fr Davy adopted, with enthusiasm, the relatively new concept of boycotting against farmers who 'broke the combination' by paying their rent, and strongly recommended that people buy only in shops displaying the Land League card. After the banning of the Land League he had founded branches of the Ladies' Land League in several parts of the county including the Hook. This often caused him to be absent from his parish from Monday to Saturday, travelling around the countryside. His influence outside Hook included the Templemore estate at Dunbrody, Clayton Brown's at Carrigbyrne, Francis Leigh's at Rosegarland and Mrs Colclough's estate at Tintern. He founded a Labourers' League to prevent labourers from co-operating with boycotted farmers. He had become a charismatic, flamboyant and imaginative leader, riding on horseback at the head of his followers, or wearing Dr Cardiff's apparel to drive into New Ross.

As the year 1881 drew to a close, Fr Davy had become a major thorn in the side of the authorities. Inquiries into his activities had been held by church and state; his arrest and that of his followers had been recommended; a meeting at the highest level in Dublin Castle had rejected that recommendation and extra troops were to be deployed to nearby Duncannon in readiness to act against him. He would have had good reason to believe that his influence was out of all proportion to his modest situation as a country curate far from the centre of power.

3. Imprisonment and evictions; the rise to prominence of Mary Anne Walsh

By 12 January 1882, 60 ejectment notices had been served on tenants on the Ely estate for Wexford quarter sessions. Taylor wrote to the chief secretary that he feared it would be most difficult to get the sub-sheriff to act because the district had become so lawless; the farmers were not working their farms; only three out of over 500 tenants had applied to the land court to fix a fair rent and very few tenants had paid.

According to Robert Kennedy RM, the majority of those served with ejectment notices on the Leigh estate at Rosegarland paid their rents on 21 January. Kennedy had been present on the day of the intended evictions but Fr Davy had not put in an appearance. The resident magistrate stayed overnight with the landlord, Francis Leigh, who gave him his opinion of the recalcitrant priest. Leigh's view was that Fr Davy's influence had greatly diminished since the bishop's reprimand and advised against arresting him. He confided to Kennedy that no one had suffered more than he had from Fr Davy's 'mischievous influence'.

Ball still seemed to be considering a prosecution against Fr Davy because he wrote to County Inspector Jones on 18 January enclosing a file from Boland. He stated that nobody would give any information on the priest unless they were assured they would not be produced as witnesses. Boland had alleged that a tenant had gone to him in disguise and told him all he knew about Fr Davy and his associates. Taylor had shown him letters from tenants with rents enclosed but begging him to serve them with writs all the same. This conflicts with Taylor's letter to the chief secretary, in which he stated that very few tenants had paid. Ball informed the county inspector that Fr Davy was on retreat at Mount Mellery, Co. Waterford. Boland continued to watch his followers and suggested that business was being transacted in the reading room while they, ostensibly, read the newspapers.

On 22 January, the under secretary was informed that Andrew Barden had succeeded in obtaining a substantial abatement of rent.[1] It seems likely that if Barden was successful, less substantial farmers were being charged an unfair rent by the marquis of Ely. On 24 January Boland informed Ball that Fr Davy was carrying on Ladies' Land League meetings through the daughters of small farmers and labourers under guise of tea parties and dances. The inspector general, G.E. Hillier, was keeping tabs on the priest, waiting for an opportunity to arrest him. On 13 February, he enquired of the under secretary if Fr

Davy and his followers were still intimidating in such a manner as would bring them under the provisions of the Protection Act.

The extra troops that had been requested do not appear to have arrived at Duncannon as, on 11 February, Taylor wrote to the chief secretary that the sheriff was unable to serve writs on the tenants because of the lack of troops. This situation was rectified and, on 16 February, the writs were executed at Fethard-on-Sea with Ball in attendance. Two days later Ball reported to Jones alleging that Fr Davy was carrying on as before but was no longer preaching. His followers put in an appearance at the execution of the writs. Nicholas Walsh was present but not Fr Davy. Another face in the crowd was that of Fr Patrick Doyle, a close friend of Fr Davy's who was curate to his uncle, Canon Tom Doyle, at Ramsgrange. At 9 o'clock that same night, Ball met Nicholas Walsh driving towards Wellington Bridge from Knocktartan. Walsh, despite having been at the Hook all day, had returned home and was, at that late hour on a winter's night, setting out on some other business. Bonfires were lit on the Hook hills to celebrate the 'No Rent' victory. Eighty soldiers and 20 policemen had accompanied the sheriff, the RM and Sub-Inspector Ball while they were executing the writs. There had been no stock or crops to seize as they had either been sold off by Nicholas Walsh at the beginning of December or were being stored with sympathetic neighbours.

Ball was summoned to the chief secretary's office on 21 February because new recommendations had been made for the arrest of several of Fr Davy's followers but not the priest himself. The chief secretary had made a decision that these arrests should be proceeded with. They included seven of the 11 previously recommended, along with two others and Fr Davy's brother, Nicholas. The nine 'suspects,' excluding Nicholas Walsh, were arrested on Sunday, 26 February by Ball with a large number of policemen and a detachment of the 37th regiment from Duncannon Fort in support. The sub-inspector had, it seems, decided to shoulder the responsibility and arrest these men himself rather than leaving it to local constables who might later be subjected to intimidation. In a report on the arrests published in the *People* newspaper, great praise was lavished on Fr Davy and regret was expressed that he had been 'forced into retirement'.[2]

Four days later, on 2 March, Nicholas O'Hanlon Walsh was arrested, on the charge of intimidation, in the home of his friend, Nicholas Furlong of Hilltown, approximately one mile from the family farm, where he had been sleeping since the eviction. Having been allowed to visit his mother and sister at the barn in Knocktartan, he was taken to Kilkenny gaol.[3] Immediately before his arrest, Nicholas Walsh had acted as auctioneer on the Boyse estate at Bannow where four ejectments had been served, and stock was sold off.[4]

On 8 March, Taylor wrote yet another complaining letter to the chief secretary claiming that the arrests had made matters worse and the animosity was now all directed towards him. He insisted he could not see anything to be gained by carrying out evictions. Kennedy, the resident magistrate, was losing patience with Taylor and, on 19 March, in a letter to the under secretary, he criticized Taylor's reluctance to complete the law proceedings 'that were commenced so forcefully'.

At this difficult time, while Fr Davy was prohibited from taking an active role in the land agitation and his brother, Nicholas, was imprisoned in Kilkenny, their sister, Mary Anne, stepped briefly into the limelight and took a leadership role. On 23 March, Taylor penned a letter to the chief secretary, registering complaints against her. He claimed that both Mary Anne and her mother had been residing with the priest since the 'final' eviction at Knocktartan. Meetings were being held at the reading room on a weekly basis, which were presided over by Miss Walsh who, he claimed, was strenuously working on the Land League programme on the Ely and adjoining estates. He presumed she was acting on the instructions of her brother. His view was that the whole Walsh family was embittered by their eviction and, because of that, they were the worst possible threat to the peace of the district.[5] This information that Mary Walsh and her daughter, Mary Anne, had been staying at Davitt Hall contradicts the report in the *People* that they were staying in the Knocktartan barn on the night of Nicholas Walsh's arrest. It is unclear what Taylor meant by the 'final' eviction but may, possibly, have referred to the date of the court case in Taghmon. The 'Land League sergeant', O'Grady, was not finally cleared from the farm until 12 April 1882.

Mary Anne Walsh seems to have been involved with both Bannow and Hook Leagues. She donated 3*s*. to the Carrig-on-Bannow and Ballymitty Prisoners' Aid Society in February, where her address was given as Knocktartan,[6] while she chaired a meeting of the Davitt Sheehy Ladies' Land League at the Hook on 5 March. At that meeting, the discussion centred on the plight of the families of the imprisoned suspects and Taylor was roundly condemned. Mary Anne Walsh addressed them saying that the good ladies of Kilkenny were looking after their prisoners and blamed Taylor for having them 'cast into gaol'. She had harsh words for the tenants on the Carrigbyrne estate of Clayton Brown remarking on how quickly they had forgotten Dr Cardiff. Two of the resolutions passed were to thank Fr Walsh for visiting the suspects in Kilkenny gaol and to congratulate Dr Cardiff on his release from prison.[7] At their next meeting on 25 March, Mary Anne Walsh presided. This meeting appears to have been a stormy one. Some fault had been found with the 'representative from Churchtown' although it is unclear as to what her crime was and her identity was not revealed in the newspaper. Mary Anne Walsh called for her removal claiming they could no longer allow her to remain a member of the executive. She spoke forcefully and emotionally about her time in the Knocktartan barn and said she had seen too much of the 'Royals' then and demanded that, as followers of Anna Parnell, they should shun all police, as if they were infected with the plague. She added that it might seem presumptuous of her to dictate to the ladies of the Hook but felt proud of the confidence they had placed in her. She assured her audience that she had no higher ambition than to carry out faithfully, to the best of her ability, the objects for which the League was founded. Her remarks about shunning the police as if they had the plague echo comments previously made by Fr Davy about shunning backsliders as they would shun patients with smallpox.[8]

At the end of March, Robert Kennedy again wrote in exasperation to the under secretary, suggesting that Taylor should deal with a few of his rich tenants as Col. Tottenham had done with the Walsh family. On 7 April, he wrote in consternation to Burke at what he saw as the surrender of Lord Templemore and Mrs Colclough on the adjoining estates of Dunbrody and Tintern. These landlords had granted their tenants 'virtually' Griffith's valuation. He intended to speak to the bishop of Ferns about having Fr Davy removed. Obviously, Kennedy saw the priest as the cause of these rent reductions. It would seem likely that Mary Anne Walsh had a hand in this also.

On 12 April, the final act in the eviction on the Knocktartan farm took place. The 'Land League sergeant' was evicted by the sheriff and resident magistrate, Kennedy. They were supported by a detachment of the 37th Regiment and several policemen. The police force entered onto the farm and drove off an ass. Emergencymen were then installed. Tottenham had requested that a couple of constables should remain on the farm but the police refused to comply.[9]

On 17 April, 11 poor tenants were evicted from a row of cottages in the village of Fethard-on-Sea, probably those renamed 'Dynamite Row' or 'Obstruction Place' by Fr Davy. For the first time since Christmas Fr Davy appeared in public, riding into the village on horseback. He asked the bailiff for his authority and added that neither the marquis nor Taylor had any authority. As he pointed out, the marquis had previously issued a circular in an attempt to come to an arrangement with his tenants. Fr Davy instructed the tenants not to give up possession until compelled to do so and advised them to hold on to the keys. He called to Taylor in the estate office, then came out and spoke to about 40 persons who had gathered and told them not to be afraid. He handed out copies of the landlord's circular and remained for about twenty minutes while the people cheered loudly.[10] The correspondent for the *People* wrote in the next issue that, in his view, these evictions had been carried out by Taylor without the consent of the marquis and that the feeling towards the agent was one of intense hatred. These poor tenants were in arrears for only the same length of time as the farmers on the estate, yet no move had been made to evict them. This correspondent had interviewed two of the evicted tenants, both named Walsh. One of them, a widow with her two married daughters and their children, told the reporter it was her third time to be evicted. She had been evicted by the previous agent, Pat Hare, uncle of Taylor, whom, she claimed, her husband had actually saved from drowning. The second interviewee was the wife of one of the imprisoned suspects who had been at work at the time the sheriff called and put her seven children out on the street. However, neighbours quickly took them in. All of the evicted, seventy persons in total, had been given shelter by their neighbours.[11] This description of the circumstances of just two of the evicted families gives an idea of the overcrowding and poverty they must have endured. The first woman had two married daughters and their children living with her, also, probably, their husbands, although they are not mentioned. In the case of the second family, where the breadwinner was in gaol, the mother had to go out to work, leaving seven children on their own in the house. The children of both families appear to have been at home and not at school, although the evictions took place on a Monday.

On 2 May, Robert Kennedy advised the chief secretary that it would be inopportune to arrest Fr Davy. He again expressed annoyance at Taylor and claimed he could have brought the tenants to their knees, like Boyse in Bannow, where, he claimed, rents were now coming in to such an extent that Ball was prepared to recommend the release of those arrested in relation to that estate. He also mentioned that he had called with the bishop of Ferns but Dr Warren said that, since Kennedy had previously been with him, he had heard nothing 'to the disadvantage of Fr Walsh'.

When rents that had been withheld began to be paid, as on the Boyse and Clayton Browne estates, those who had been imprisoned as the suspected agitators were deemed eligible for release. This happened in the case of Dr Joe Cardiff on the Clayton Browne estate and James Ennis and Denis Crosbie on the Boyse estate. Surprisingly, as rents continued to be withheld on the Ely estate, five of the suspects were released from Kilkenny Gaol on 14 and 15 June, followed by two more on 17 June. It would appear that the remaining two, apart from Nicholas Walsh, had already been released, possibly on grounds of ill health. There is no correspondence on the file relating to the reasons for their release or on the actual releases. In any event, the men returned home to Fethard-on-Sea amid great celebration and proceeded to the home of one of the suspects, Mathew Foley, which was a public house. Fr Davy had met them in Waterford and accompanied them by boat to Ballyhack and on to Fethard. About 2,000 supporters were there to welcome them, it was reported, and there was a notable absence of police. Mathew Foley spoke eloquently from a window of his house. His new-found oratorical skill astounded the next speaker, Fr Patrick Doyle, who suggested that Kilkenny gaol had acted as a college in developing 'a silent worker into an eloquent advocate of popular rights'. When it was recalled that Fr Davy was unable to participate in political affairs, 'a momentary gloom was cast' on the proceedings.[12]

Another occasion for great rejoicing was the return home of Nicholas Walsh on Sunday, 9 July, having been released from prison three weeks previously. The *People* newspaper began referring to him as 'The O'Hanlon

Walsh'. A procession accompanied him from the Hook to his newly con-
structed 'Land League cottage' in Ballymitty. Thousands marched along
waving flags and banners, and hundreds of sympathisers gathered at crossroads
and along the route of the parade, which was said to be two and a half miles
in length. Flags of green and gold were everywhere, arches spanned the road
at intervals and almost every cottage was decorated with flowers and green
boughs. Women along the route presented Nicholas Walsh with bouquets. He
had been staying with Fr Davy at Davitt Hall since his release, awaiting the
completion of his new home. He had leased approximately 15 acres in the
townland of Ballymitty some years previously and it was on this land that
Carrig-on-Bannow Land League had built his cottage.[13] Crowds came from
all over south Wexford to welcome him home. They had begun arriving at
Davitt Hall at 1.00 p.m. where they were treated hospitably by Fr Davy. They
were invited to inspect the saddle and bridle which had been a gift to the
priest from the Boston Land League, which may have been intended as a
compliment to his well-known skill in horsemanship. He was unable to accom-
pany the procession because of the restrictions placed on him. At 2.30 p.m.,
headed by the Ballymitty fife and drum band, dressed in neat uniforms the
procession moved off, playing 'national' airs. A special feature was a wagonette
drawn by two horses from which hung a green flag. On the flag was displayed
a representation of the 'harp without the crown'. Nicholas Walsh and the nine
other suspects took their place in this wagon while in the two cars following
them, were Dr Joe Cardiff and James Ennis, both recently released prisoners.
The parade took four and a half hours to travel the twelve miles to Ballymitty
and arrived at 7.00 p.m. A deafening cheer arose when they came within sight
of the Land League cottage where the women of Carrig-on-Bannow branch
had assembled to welcome 'the League auctioneer'. Dr Cardiff spoke from a
window and praised Nicholas Walsh and the men of Hook. Someone called
for a leader like Fr Davy, which resulted in loud cheers for the priest. Mathew
Foley acknowledged the compliment paid to the Hook men but attributed their
determined attitude to the teaching of their own Fr Davy. When Nicholas Walsh
appeared he was loudly applauded. He made a short speech in which he declared
he would continue to be the sworn enemy of tyranny and oppression. At the
end the band played 'God save Ireland,' which, during this period, was often
referred to as the Irish National Anthem and 'The Boys of Wexford,' after
which the crowds dispersed.[14] Even allowing for exaggeration, this must have
been an incredible spectacle, with the crowds, the music, the flags and the
flowers. It must surely have moved Nicholas Walsh deeply. However, he
appears to have lacked the charisma of his brother, Fr Davy. There are no
reports of wild cheering or ovations when he spoke. We are simply told that
he gave a 'brief speech'.

On 8 May, the marquis of Ely sent a further circular to his tenants offering
a permanent reduction in rent of 20 per cent. However, this would not

include recent lettings, leaseholds, monthly and weekly tenants and houses in Fethard-on-Sea.[15] On 16 August he again communicated with them stating that his proposal had not had the desired effect and that he was directing his agent to collect his rents without further delay. On 30 August, Godfrey Taylor advised the chief secretary that evictions would go ahead and requested that the barony of Shelburne be proclaimed. He stated that Fr Davy continued to influence events. On 5 September, in a memo to Robert Kennedy, the resident magistrate, the chief secretary criticised Taylor for not taking action against his wealthy tenants and asked Kennedy's opinion on the proposed proclamation of Shelburne. Kennedy informed the under secretary that he was in agreement with it.[16] The final document in this correspondence is a telegram, dated 16 September 1882. It informed the inspector general that County Inspector Jones had heard a number of those tenants to be evicted had paid, and that as many as were able would do so in advance of the sheriff's arrival. No opposition was anticipated.

The evictions and seizure of stock occurred over four days, commencing on 19 September. According to a letter published by the *People*, it would appear that 18 tenants were evicted while a further seven paid up when the sheriff arrived, or shortly afterwards. In six of these cases, stock had been seized and, in order to reclaim it, the rent was paid. In the seventh case, the tenant promised to pay as soon as his pigs were fattened and this was accepted. For some unknown reason, four others who refused to pay were not evicted.[17] Fr Davy does not appear to have been present at any of these evictions. The tone of the above letter appears to have upset another *People* reader, who replied signing himself 'a Tenant'. He claimed the tenants who paid were perfectly entitled to do so and that the 'No Rent Manifesto,' having done its work, had long since been withdrawn. He stated that those tenants who paid did so with the sanction of Canon Doyle of Ramsgrange.[18]

In a further veiled attack on Fr Walsh and his brother, the same *nom-de-plume:* 'a Tenant' was used in a letter published on 11 October. This time he was defending Andrew Barden, poor law rate collector. He stated that Barden could not pledge himself to suffer eviction if the tenants' demands were not conceded and would not be one to allow 'a colourable sale by auction of his cattle to the tune of tin whistle and drum, with green flags floating on the breeze in his yard'. Andrew Barden himself may well have been the author of these letters. This correspondence gives us an indication that a split in the ranks of the tenants on the estate of the marquis of Ely had developed. It would appear that those who supported Fr Davy were on one side while their opponents were backed by Canon Tom Doyle.

As one of the instigators of the Land League in Co. Wexford, Canon Tom Doyle's letter published in the *People* on 28 October is very surprising. It was almost obsequious in its praise of the marquis of Ely and his agent, Taylor. He praised them for their 'benevolence towards the Hook tenantry'. He claimed that the tenants had been given an abatement of 20 per cent, not only his yearly tenants but also those who were bound by lease, some of whom were very wealthy. However, this is patently untrue since the circular issued to the tenants on 8 May clearly excluded leaseholds from the 20 per cent reduction. Canon Doyle declared that he considered the demands of the Hook tenantry to be very unreasonable. He said he had tried to indicate this at the Poulfur meeting, presumably a year previously, on 29 September 1881, but, he claimed, 'other counsels prevailed to the great loss and annoyance of all concerned'. This is surely a reference to Fr Davy. Finally, he advised tenants who could not afford to pay rent to put their cases to Mr Taylor whose response Canon Doyle expected would be magnanimous.[19]

The year 1882 was not such a good one for Fr Davy. He had been prevented from preaching or taking any part in politics. He seems to have obeyed his bishop's orders, with the single exception of the first day of the evictions of the poor tenants in Fethard village. He was probably unable to resist the urge to intervene on their behalf on that occasion. He did have some gains, in relation to the Templemore and Colclough estates, whose tenants procured abatements almost equal to Griffith's valuation. Equally though, it appears that the tenants of Leigh of Rosegarland and probably also Clayton Brown's at Carrigbyrne paid up, if one considers Mary Anne Walsh's remark about them forgetting Dr Cardiff very quickly. The tenants on the Boyse estate at Bannow also paid, although Fr Davy appears to have had little involvement with them. Sadly, a split was developing among his followers, tenants on the Ely estate. Some had paid up but many were still resisting and had been evicted. Andrew Barden, with the support of Canon Doyle, was possibly stirring up trouble. Barden had been the first to 'break the combination' by applying to the Land Court to fix his rent. He was successful in gaining an abatement and paid his rent. He had suffered ostracization at the hands of Fr Davy and had taken his revenge by informing the police of the forthcoming auction and by giving testimony to the bishop in relation to Fr Davy's activities. The priest was able to join in the celebrations on the release of the prisoners, including his brother, but was not allowed to attend the public gatherings arranged for them.

Nicholas Walsh, having spent over three months in Kilkenny gaol had come home to the gift of a newly built cottage and a hero's welcome. The brothers were lucky to have had their sister, Mary Anne, ready to step into the breach in order to carry on their work. She appears to have been an articulate speaker, perhaps more along the lines of Fr Davy rather than Nicholas, who appeared to keep his public speaking to a minimum.

4. Tensions in two communities

By October 1882, a collection to provide a testimonial for Nicholas O'Hanlon Walsh had been underway for some time. At an interim meeting of the committee elected to collect subscriptions towards it, those who had so far subscribed were listed. They came from all over south Co. Wexford but mainly from Bannow and the Hook. A letter and subscription was received from Fr Patrick Doyle, nephew of Canon Doyle and close friend of Fr Davy. In his letter he praised the O'Hanlon Walsh family profusely for its 'huge contribution to the cause of land law reform'. He regretted there weren't more tenants like them and expressed the belief that, if there had been, landlordism would already have been overthrown. He referred to the costs that must have accumulated to Col Tottenham, in relation to the Knocktartan farm since their eviction, involving writs, law and sheriff's expenses, wages, provisions, tobacco and 'stimulants' for the emergencymen and the carriage of these provisions, and so on.[1] In early March 1883, at a further meeting of this committee, it was decided to close the fund at Easter.[2]

On 1 April the address and testimonial were presented to Nicholas at his new home. Edward Walsh, editor of the *People* and chairman of the organizing committee, was in attendance, as were many large tenant farmers from the parish and surrounding districts, as well as Michael Browne, chairman of Wexford board of guardians. Speeches were made by Edward Walsh and Michael Browne and a purse of gold was presented to Nicholas. He replied that their cause, although not yet successful, was now on the 'high road to success'. The address was illuminated by Henry Leary of Wexford. On the top centre was the Walsh coat of arms bearing the motto, 'Death before dishonour'. On the right was a sketch of the family home at Knocktartan and, on the left a sketch of Land League cottage. At the bottom centre was the figure of Erin, very popular in the Parnell era. On the right was a representation of Davitt Hall, the home of Fr Davy while a sketch of the 'Land League mare', which the sheriff had been unable to remove from Knocktartan on the day of the eviction in June 1881, featured on the bottom left of the address. The evening ended in the cottage's 'snug little parlour' where several songs were sung.[3]

In the autumn of 1882, Parnell had disbanded the Land League and established in its place the Irish National League. The aims of the new organization were more political than agrarian, the main objective being to assist the Home Rule movement. On 7 January 1883, a branch of the new organization was established at Land League cottage, Ballymitty, the home of Nicholas O'Hanlon Walsh. A large number attended the meeting and a committee was elected which included Nicholas. The Ballymitty fife and drum band rendered a selection of 'national' airs. Three members of the RIC kept the proceedings under surveillance.[4] At their second meeting, held at the same venue on 11 February, the rules of the organization were read, along with circulars from central branch. A resolution was passed, calling on the government to provide plots of land and suitable houses for the labourers.[5]

A branch of the Irish National League had also been established at the Hook and, at their meeting of 9 June, deep regret was expressed at the absence of Fr Davy whose assistance, it was claimed, was most needful. This was a crushing blow to his faithful followers but they were consoled that he was with them in spirit for, it was declared, 'a more pure souled patriot did not exist on the sacred soil of Ireland'.[6]

At the September 1883 meeting of Carrig-on-Bannow National League many labourers were in attendance and some enrolled as members in anticipation of the Labourers' (Ireland) Act being passed. It was resolved that the Act would be worked in its entirety in the parish, with as little delay as possible. All labourers and those who took an interest in labourers' welfare were requested to attend a special meeting to be convened on 16 September in order to give consideration to the labour question. It was noted that the labourer was 'the real bone and sinew of the land'.[7] In October, a great county meeting of the National League was held at Wexford town at which Michael Davitt and several MPs were present. Several members of the clergy attended but there was no sign of Fr Davy. The Ballymitty fife and drum band headed a large contingent from Bannow.[8]

Supporters of Fr Davy had decided to honour him as his brother had been honoured and began taking subscriptions for a testimonial to acknowledge his contribution in late 1883. Collections were confined mainly to the Hook and the presentation was made to him on New Year's Day, 1884. It was an amazing presentation – an illuminated address, set in a heavy gilt frame, with his own photograph at the top and those of Parnell and Davitt at either side of him. At the bottom was the Walsh family arms and crest. This was the work of Lynch of Middle Abbey Street, Dublin. The testimonial consisted of a purse of sovereigns, a wagonette croydon and a set of silver mounted harness. According to the report, the croydon, by Leary of Wexford, and the harness, by Hore of Wexford, were wonderful specimens of workmanship. The croydon was painted dark green and was upholstered in green and gold cloth. Both the croydon and harness bore the Walsh family crest – a forearm with the hand grasping a tilting spear. The chairman of the organizing committee said the people of Hook wished to recognise the services that Fr Davy had rendered to them over the past few years. He had stood beside them in their struggle to gain the right to live in their own country and to own the soil they tilled. The address was even more glowing, singling him out, above all the clergy, for standing by the people. There was a warning for priests in general that the tie between priest and people was loosening rapidly and it wasn't the fault of the people. However, if other priests were to imitate Fr Davy, the bonds would become stronger than ever. The priest responded appropriately. Six hundred parishioners were assembled outside when they emerged while the committee and friends of Fr Davy's were invited to dinner in Davitt Hall.[9]

As 1883 drew to a close in the parish of Bannow, sites for labourers' cottages with gardens were being promised by several large tenant farmers.[10] In November, in Ballymitty electoral division, a row developed over the allocation of two sites for labourers' cottages on the Walsh evicted farm at Knocktartan.[11] The sites were chosen by Adam O'Neill, poor law guardian for the division. Michael Browne, Bridgetown, chairman of the board of guardians, recommended that these sites be changed because no respectable labourer would take a house built on Knocktartan. He suggested four other alternative farms and this suggestion was adopted unanimously by the board. Adam O'Neill, also a tenant of Col. Tottenham,[12] in the adjoining parish of Taghmon, was not present at the meeting.[13] O'Neill's actions were condemned at the December meeting of Carrig-on-Bannow National League while Michael Browne was praised as a man of 'independent principles and an opponent of all supporters of felonious landlordism'.[14]

By February 1884, Carrig-on-Bannow National League was occupied with the election of the poor law guardian for the Ballymitty electoral division and was calling on the ratepayers to support a nationalist against the incumbent, Adam O'Neill, at the forthcoming March election. The candidate they selected was John McCormack of Arnestown, a townland adjoining Knocktartan. Ballymitty electoral division included a substantial part of the parish of Taghmon as well as Ballymitty and Ballingly. On 9 February, at a hearing of Wexford board of guardians, Thomas Boyd, Col. Tottenham's agent, objected to one of the proposed alternative sites recommended by Michael Browne. This site was situated on the farm of John Doran of Knocktartan, another tenant of Tottenham. Boyd was accompanied by Adam O'Neill who declared that the four sites accepted by the Board were unsuitable as compared with the ones chosen by him on the Walsh evicted farm. O'Neill claimed to have the sanction of the ratepayers. His objection to the alternative sites was that they were too close to the farmers' houses. For example, the one proposed for John Doran's farm was at the entrance to his haggard. Boyd agreed with O'Neill. Browne repeated his contention that houses built on a boycotted farm would not be taken by labourers. Enoch Richards, another farmer, though not a tenant of Tottenham's, deposed that his mother was tenant of the lands at Ballymitty crossroads and that the site proposed for their property would be on their cabbage-garden and within twenty perches of their residence. The proximity of the cottage would interfere with their dwelling house, which was also a public house. Thomas Culleton, poor law guardian for Harristown electoral division, announced that he was providing a site on his own farm as close to his house as that of the Richards and expressed the opinion that a cottage built near a public house would not do any harm.[15] In the event, the only labourer's cottage to be actually built on Knocktartan townland was erected on Dorans' farm, but not until *c*.1894, ten years after this dispute arose. A cottage was built on Richards' land in 1889.[16]

On 16 February, a letter bearing the *nom-de-plume* 'Veritas' was published in the *People*. In this letter the Walsh family was lauded for standing by their principles and refusing to pay a rack-rent, which was 30 per cent over Griffith's valuation. Adam O'Neill was condemned for 'standing in the Wexford Boardroom beside an evicting agent' and it concluded that the people would remember this at the forthcoming election.[17] A ballad, or part of a ballad, survives which deals with the eviction of 'Widow Walsh'. At first glance one would assume it to have been written shortly after that event. However, knowledge of the dispute relating to the sites for labourers and the poor law guardian election throws a somewhat different light on the ballad and suggests that it wasn't written until early 1884. It was likely to have been used as an instrument of propaganda in the election campaign and, indeed, may have been written for that very purpose. I quote here in full what survives of the ballad:

A Land League Song

There was a wealthy farmer lived convenient to this place
He went against his neighbours and sank into disgrace
He went against his neighbours, a thing he should avoid
He gained a lad from Chilcomb Lodge whose name was Thomas Boyd.

This boy he was an agent as you may plainly see
He evicted the poor Widow Walsh, likewise her family
He left them all without a roof, the truth I'll not deny
He was backed up by a farmer, his name was Adam Neill.

Long life to John McCormack who boldly fought the cause
And to the Ballymitty boys who should get great applause
Likewise poor Willie McCoy, we will not him forget
He lived upon the cross going up to Big Slevoy.[18]

The wealthy farmer, in the first line, is obviously the landlord, Tottenham, whose agent was Thomas Boyd. The impression given in the ballad is that Widow Walsh was a poor woman who could not afford to pay her rent and who was left 'without a roof'. The last line of the second stanza and the first line of the third particularly suggest that the ballad was written in early 1884. 'He was backed up by a farmer, his name was Adam Neill' echoes the letter previously mentioned which condemned Adam O'Neill for 'standing in Wexford Boardroom beside an evicting agent'. John McCormack was the candidate chosen by the local branch of the National League to stand for election as poor law guardian. McCormack is named and lauded while Adam O'Neill is named and condemned and stripped of the Irish prefix 'O' in his surname. However, in Co. Wexford, up to recent years, the prefix 'O' was often dropped, for no apparent reason, so too much significance should not be placed on that.

Despite the efforts of the League, when the election came around, Adam O'Neill won the election by 66 votes to 55. Many of the electors held more than one vote – 41 people voted for O'Neill while 36 voted for McCormack. More of the wealthier farmers voted for O'Neill. For example, Adam O'Neill himself had four votes while John McCormack had only two. It is interesting that John Doran and Moses Ennis, two of the three tenants remaining on Knocktartan townland, voted for O'Neill while the third, James McGrath, voted for McCormack. Nicholas O'Hanlon Walsh, as one might expect, also voted for McCormack.[19]

At the April meeting of the Hook branch, Fr Davy made his re-appearance and was scathing of the choice of the Ballymitty electors. Having been silenced by Bishop Warren in late 1881, he began to participate in politics again in April 1884. By the time he attended this meeting, Bishop Warren was seriously ill and he died on 22 April.[20] His death would appear to have allowed for Fr Davy's re-involvement. He declared, at that meeting, that Ballymitty had scored a brilliant success 'on behalf of the exterminators – the natural effect of that over-prudence for which Carrig-on-Bannow is now so famous'. Carrig-on-Bannow League expressed regret that 'the minions of landlordism have so many supporters among the tenant farmers of Ballymitty division'. Nicholas O'Hanlon Walsh and Denis Crosbie were selected by Carrig-on-Bannow branch to attend the Co. Wexford convention later that month, the purpose of which was to discuss a plan for payment of MPs. Fr Davy was present at the convention, along with other delegates from the Hook. He expressed the view that landlords should be left without rent in order to pay the members. His resolution was carried. A banquet was held afterwards in honour of John and William Redmond, both MPs for Co. Wexford. The O'Hanlon Walsh brothers attended, as did Dr Joe Cardiff.[21]

By June, Fr Davy was back chairing meetings of Hook National League but his re-involvement there was to be short-lived. When Dr James Browne was consecrated bishop of Ferns on 14 September, Fr Davy's name was missing from the long list of priests who attended the ceremony. On 1 November the new bishop transferred him from Hook to Castlebridge, near Wexford town.[22] When the news broke there was consternation among his followers in the Hook. They refused to accept the bishop's decision and proceeded to nail up the door of Templetown church. Canon Tom Doyle, years later, claimed that they also nailed up the door of the parochial house, Davitt Hall, to prevent the newly-appointed curate, Fr John Lyng, from gaining admittance.[23] This state of affairs continued until the bishop partially relented three months later, on 1 February 1885 by transferring Fr Lyng to

Bunclody.[24] Fr Lyng had actually spent two years in Hook parish previously, as assistant to his uncle, Canon James Lyng PP, at Poulfur.[25] Fr Hanly, a native of Co. Tipperary, replaced him. Canon Doyle claimed that, when Fr Hanly arrived, the locals unbarred the church door because there were 'rumours' that the parish would be placed 'under an interdict'. This meant exclusion from certain sacraments, though not from communion. However, the parochial house remained barred for some time thereafter forcing the young priest to take lodgings with a farmer in nearby Galgystown. This episode shows that, in the nineteenth century, ordinary country people, farmers and labourers, were not afraid to defy the clergy and, even the bishop was not held in awe. They were also not so afraid of hell-fire as to worry about the consequences for their souls of preventing a large number of people from attending Mass for three whole months.

At the November 1884 meeting of Hook National League, a resolution had been passed declaring that all the parishioners were 'in mourning' for the loss of their 'zealous and pious priest, a sterling tried-and-true Irishman, Rev. David O'Hanlon Walsh'. They poured scorn on his opponents within the parish, calling them 'upholders of Castle rule' and 'priest-maligning wretches'. They stated that these opponents thought that Dillon Place was silenced and the Hook 200 dead. However, they were there to prove they were still living and vigorous.[26]

In this chapter there is evidence of much acclaim being accorded to the O'Hanlon Walsh brothers and it cannot be denied that they had friends and supporters all over Co. Wexford. However, there were, likewise, many who opposed them and the aims of the Irish National League. This is evidenced in John McCormack's election defeat by Adam O'Neill. Even if each person voting had only one vote each, O'Neill would still have won by a margin of five votes. Two out of three of the tenants on Knocktartan townland voted for O'Neill, including the Walshs' cousins. One has to bear in mind, though, that the greater part of Ballymitty electoral division was located in the parish of Taghmon where O'Neill lived and this cannot be ruled out as a factor in his victory. Parish loyalties, then, as now, were likely to have been quite strong, even before the rise of the GAA. There may have been an even simpler explanation. Those tenants from Taghmon parish who voted for O'Neill were all tenants of Tottenham, as were those on Knocktartan townland, as well as O'Neill himself. Perhaps the landlord still held sway with many of his tenants or, possibly, some inducement was offered. The dispute about the location of labourers' cottages, and tensions between the tenant farmers, probably delayed the construction of any cottages, in these townlands, for several years. The protest was, of course, successful in preventing cottages from being erected on the Walsh family farm. Finally, the loyalty to Fr Davy of the great majority of people in the Hook meant they were prepared to go to any lengths to keep him with them, even to defying the new bishop.

5. The Revd David O'Hanlon Walsh in Wexford town and his brief return to the Hook

Tensions in Ballymitty had not eased since the poor law guardian election in March. In July 1884, objections were raised in relation to a tenant farmer in Knocktartan having 'grabbed' manure from the evicted farm for his own use and also to him having become a herd on that farm. These actions were condemned at Carrig-on-Bannow's July meeting.[1] The condemnation was quickly followed by the publication of a letter in the next edition of the *People*, signed with the *nom-de-plume* of 'Outsider'. This letter eulogised the Walsh family, and particularly Mary Walsh, 'who was prepared to give up her home for a principle'. The author also condemned the conduct of the tenant farmer.[2] Another letter, using the *nom-de-plume* 'Hibernicus' appeared in the edition of the *People* of 11 July, this time purporting to be from an exile who had recently returned to Ireland after several years absence. The returned exile had gone 'hot foot' to Knocktartan, having followed its story in the newspapers. The Walsh family was again eulogised. These letters may have been written either by members of the Walsh family or close friends and supporters of theirs. They appeared at intervals, either to air a particular grievance, or, more generally, to keep the case and the cause of the Walsh family alive in the public consciousness. It must have been galling for them to realize that they had allowed themselves to be evicted only to find their neighbours were turning their backs on them.

In March 1885, at his second attempt, John McCormack was returned as poor law guardian for Ballymitty, defeating Adam O'Neill. An inquiry into the validity of the election was subsequently held where the votes of one person who opted for McCormack were disallowed but he still emerged the winner by a margin of just two votes – 72 to 70. Unfortunately, details of the voting are not provided as they were in 1884 so it is not possible to see who had a change of heart.[3]

A great demonstration was held at Taghmon in May 1885 at which three MPs, William Redmond, Barry and Small were present. Redmond called for boycotting. Only one priest was in attendance because a new rule had been introduced preventing priests from attending public meetings. However, just as the crowds were beginning to disperse, Fr Davy made his entrance. He had been a curate in Wexford town since March. On seeing him, the crowds remained to give him 'a hearty welcome'. Three bands escorted him to the hotel, playing 'See the conquering hero come'.[4]

In June and July 1885 there was further condemnation of the tenant on the Knocktartan estate by Carrig-on-Bannow National League. It was claimed that his family was friendly to an emergencyman from Duncormack on the occasions when he came to look after the cattle on the evicted farm. He was also accused of keeping an eye on the cattle in the emergencyman's absence and the League described the tenant's brother-in-law as the 'deputy emergencyman' and thanked John Murphy of Kilcavan for refusing him the services of his bull.[5]

In September, at a great demonstration at Rosemount (Drinagh), near Wexford town, Fr Davy was very much in evidence and other priests were also present. The ban on priests attending public meetings would appear to have been lifted. As previously stated, Fr Davy was now serving as a curate in Wexford town and, mindful of his new urban posting, he spoke to the assembled gathering on behalf of 'nationalist' shopkeepers. These were shopkeepers who displayed the membership card of the Irish National League. He accused his audience of frequenting anti-national and anti-Irish shops in Wexford town while nationalist shops were being ignored. He claimed they were doing this despite having passed resolutions to have no dealings with those who did not support the cause. He spoke of ladies of the county wishing to acquire the particular shade of green worn by the princess of Wales on a recent visit to Ireland. This shade was available in only one or two shops and nobody was left in any doubt that these were not nationalist shops. He stated that he had been honoured with membership of many of the executives of the county and promised to bring it to the attention of the appropriate executive if members were seen to be frequenting those shops.[6] While he was not exactly advocating the boycotting of non-nationalist shops, he was certainly recommending exclusive dealing.

Shortly afterwards, he was elected an honorary member of Wexford National League in the presence of William Redmond MP when he delivered a similar speech to the one he had given at Drinagh. He indicated his anti-sectarianism by declaring that he did not care 'three jackstraws whether a shopkeeper was Catholic, Protestant or heretic, the only criterion was the card of membership of the National League.'[7] This trend of electing Fr Davy as an honorary member was continued by Taghmon National League in September and Carrig-on-Bannow in October.[8] He began showing up at meetings and demonstrations all around the county. In October he was one of the main speakers at a great meeting in Rathnure where he declared that leaguers were being chastized for their unchristian-like practice of boycotting. He asked, rhetorically, who had taught them how to boycott – the authorities had boycotted Catholics from the bench and every office it was in their power to confer.[9]

In late November, at a demonstration at Ballymurn, near Enniscorthy, attended by thousands, he told his listeners that it would be a fatal mistake at any time or in any crisis to rely too much on any one individual. Perhaps he was reflecting here that, maybe, his followers in the Hook had relied too heavily on him.[10] In December, he was present at Crossabeg League meeting where he gave a lengthy address and at Wexford where he proposed that a district council of surrounding branches be formed. This proposal was adopted.[11]

On 7 January 1886, he again played a prominent role at a meeting of Wexford National League. A tenant who had been served with an eviction notice came before the committee. Fr Davy advised him to get the board to build a labourer's cottage on his farm and, if he was evicted, he could move into the cottage and suggested that no other tenant would dare to 'grab' the farm while he was living on it. The priest appeared to have an easy, relaxed exchange with the tenant and seemed genuinely sympathetic. He reiterated the need to purchase from League members and to choose Irish produce. He insisted that boycotting was the only way to succeed in their 'desperate struggle'.[12]

At the Wexford meeting of 3 February, he began promoting cottage industry, particularly in relation to 'bottle-envelopes' made of straw. These envelopes were being manufactured around Bridgetown and Kilmore and were used to contain bottles of spirits. Fr Davy encouraged those in the liquor trade to purchase their envelopes from French & Browne of Bridgetown rather than placing their orders in France or England. Browne of Bridgetown may well have been Michael Browne, chairman of Wexford board of guardians, or a member of his family. Fr Davy believed cottage industry would be an opportunity for evicted families to earn a living rather than being obliged to beg. He then turned to the appalling housing conditions prevailing in Wexford town, which he sarcastically referred to as 'the model town of the Model County'. He had visited rooms in the back streets and lanes of the town that were not fit for dogs to sleep in. He scorned the 'so-called moral obligation' of paying the exorbitant rent that was being demanded for these 'dens'. He related an incident where a neighbour had to come into such a room to rock a cradle while the mother went to pawn her last dress in order to find one shilling and sixpence to pay the rent for her miserable little room. He called on the commissioners to build decent houses for the people forced to live in these 'cells'. Peter O'Dwyer of Main Street proposed a motion that it was time to establish a House league (presumably an urban equivalent of Land League). William Kehoe, a labourer, seconded the motion. The president, Edward Walsh, said the proposal was one that ought to receive no opposition but he favoured it being part of the National League. He referred to a particular eviction that was pending in the town but, because the tenant had not authorized anyone to bring it forward, said it might be as well not to raise the issue. However, Fr Davy showed an understanding of the difficulties that would face such a woman in bringing it forward and suggested that she would feel she had no one to look out for her. He stressed that they must make it known that Wexford League intended to look after the interests of the poor and to ensure that they would not pay an exorbitant rent or live in houses unfit for habitation. He was hopeful that a large number of working people would swell the ranks. A committee, which included Fr Davy, was appointed to inquire into and report on all matters connected with the House league.[13] The indefatigable priest attended the New Ross local convention of the National League that same month and was scathing of the town's failure to stop purchasing milk from evicted farms. There was a considerable amount of dissension between various parties at the convention, the chairman insisting that it was very difficult for New Ross, where only about 400 people were members of the League out of a population of 6,000 to 7,000 inhabitants.[14]

As far back as April 1885, a circular had been received from Castlebridge by Carrig-on-Bannow National League asking them to co-operate in raising a further testimonial to Fr Davy. They wanted to make up for the poor treatment he had received for his unselfish devotion to the cause of Irish nationalism.[15] Since then, subscriptions had continued to flow in and on Monday, 21 February 1886, an address and testimonial was presented to him at the family home – Land League Cottage, Ballymitty. That this testimonial was initiated by the people of Castlebridge was remarkable – he had spent only four months as their curate before being transferred to Wexford on 1 March 1885. The chairman on the day was his old friend, Dr Joe Cardiff. Three bands accompanied the procession from Wexford: the Wexford National League band, the Castlebridge band and the Johnstown fife and drum band. Dr Cardiff told them that when he was a prisoner in Kilmainham gaol he had ensured that the name of Fr Davy was as well known to the prisoners from Connacht and Kerry as he was known at home in Wexford. Fr Davy was presented with a purse embroidered in green and gold. His address to the gathering, delivered in his native place, was reflective and tinged with sadness. He declared that, if his family had to go out again, out they would go. He recalled that many of those present had attended the eviction and some had cried when a few gallons of buttermilk were spilled. He remembered the crowds on the famous harvesting day when things had looked bright. However, time had passed and the clouds had darkened. He, himself, had been prevented from taking part in political affairs, while his brother, Nick, had been lodged in Kilkenny Gaol. He asked the men of Ballymitty where they were then and where his next-door neighbours and cousins had been. He answered, sadly, that they were herding the cattle for Tom Boyd on the Walsh farm. Then, when Tom Boyd was anxious to build a couple of cottages on the farm, the men of Ballymitty had dried their tears, forgot the spilt milk and returned Adam O'Neill as poor law guardian. He demanded that John McCormack be returned again this year, as he was last year, so that the Leighs, the Boyds and the O'Neills might not 'win their spurs'. He called for their support for Irish manufactured goods. He said every gallon of whiskey drunk gave twelve shillings to the government, yet some tenants were reluctant to pay out of the rates the cost for the labourers' cottages. He again condemned Andrew Barden of Fethard, who appears to have become his *bête noir*, this time for being involved in coursing. Dr Cardiff, speaking at the conclusion, said he wished to honour the ladies, as it was 'not yet fashionable' for them to speak in public, despite their eloquence. He wanted to say that their record in the struggle was first-class. He claimed that in recent years when the Land League was suppressed, many men who had loudly talked of pikes and rebellion had slunk into a mouse-hole. Then the ladies came to the fore and formed the Ladies' Land League and did their work far better than many men would have done it. The evening concluded, as usual, with the playing of 'God save Ireland'.[16]

A couple of weeks before Fr Davy was presented with this second testimonial, a great open-air demonstration was held at Templetown under the auspices of the Hook branch on 7 February. The state of the roads, after a night of heavy rain, prevented many people from travelling. A vast number of RIC men were present. Nicholas O'Hanlon Walsh was there, undeterred by the weather. The object of the meeting was to enable the tenants on the Ely estate to claim the necessary abatement in their rent; to promote and facilitate the erection of labourers' cottages in the parish; to extend the organization of the National League, so as to embrace everyone of 'national feelings and aspirations' in the parish. Two of the apologies received were from Fr Thomas Meehan CC, Ballymitty and Canon Tom Doyle PP, Ramsgrange. Fr Meehan cautioned against the use of 'extravagance of language or actions,' advised that no resolutions of boycotting be proposed and called on the tenants to be united. Canon Doyle also called for the establishment of unity among the Hook tenantry. These two priests may have deliberately absented themselves from the meeting knowing that Fr Davy was to attend and the apologies included subtle warnings to him not to overstep the mark. Fr Patrick Doyle, nephew of Canon Tom and friend of Fr Davy, chaired the meeting. He declared that, if Ireland had followed the example of the Hook in 1881-2, the tenants of Hook would not be back today seeking an abatement. He praised those who had supported the tenants, making particular mention of the Davitt Sheehy Ladies' Land League who 'stood nobly in the shoes of the men'. He mentioned, above all, the man who was always to be found 'in the gap if danger was near,' none other than Fr Davy. When the man in question stepped forward to speak, there was a storm of cheering, and a waving of hats and handkerchiefs, which lasted several minutes. He spoke briefly, on this first return visit, stating that many had thought their demands extravagant in 1881–2 but now had come to realise their practicality. A dinner was held afterwards at 6, Dillon Place where photographs of military raids and electoral achievements adorned the walls. Fr Doyle was again in the chair and proposed the health of Fr Davy. When he arose to return thanks, he was again met with rapturous applause.[17]

On 8 March, a meeting of the tenants on the Ely estate was held and Fr Davy was again to the forefront. He informed the tenants that he was there by the kind permission of their parish priest to give them any assistance he could. (Fr Richard Kelly still remained parish priest of Hook parish.)[18] He told them there was only one thing that could defeat them – treachery and disunity in their ranks. He made a very personal attack on Andrew Barden, accusing him of being the individual who had caused disunity in the ranks in 1881–2. He accused Barden of going behind backs in order to secure himself with the landlord and contemptuously described him as director of the coursing club. The priest said he was hearing a lot about forgiveness, peace and unity. However, that should not mean that honest men had to stand aside and make way for 'flunkeys', because men like Barden wanted to be at the helm. He advised them not to be afraid of eviction, only the grabber was to be feared. He said, obviously referring to the situation of his own family, that life in a cabin was not so bad if one could keep an eye on the old homestead.[19]

After this meeting, Fr Davy appears to have become inactive again. On 2 May, at the next meeting of the tenantry, Canon Doyle was the main speaker while Fr Davy was notably absent. It is likely that Canon Doyle had refused to share a platform with him and, possibly, some manoeuvring had gone on to put the Canon in control of events. He made a very pointed remark, early in his speech, about knowing the Ely tenantry longer than any priest in the diocese of Ferns. He was quite condescending towards them and again sang the praises of the marquis of Ely. He said he was convinced the marquis would grant them their demand of 25 per cent reduction. He spoke of his very high opinion of Godfrey Taylor and admonished the tenants for being unreasonable in 1881–2. He declared that, if he had been asked to arbitrate, he would not have acceded to their request. He reminded them that Archbishop Croke of Cashel had condemned the 'No Rent Manifesto'. Fr Patrick Doyle, his nephew, rather surprisingly, because of his acknowledged admiration for Fr Davy and his family and his remarks at the previous meeting, agreed with Canon Doyle and told the tenants that they had got Griffith's valuation. Somebody shouted: 'But we had the best of a leader'. Fr Doyle agreed that they had a leader deserving of their 'everlasting respect,' but that he would not be prepared to stand by everything that leader had said. However, he did believe him to be honest, self-sacrificing and sincere, although he had made errors of judgment in his methods of action, but he did so 'through an honest purpose.' A representative for each townland was appointed which included Andrew Barden.[20] These remarks by Fr Doyle make his earlier praise of Fr Davy, at the February meeting, sound hollow and hypocritical. He may, of course, have feared his uncle and have been under strict instructions to 'toe the line'.

Sadly for the Ely tenants, Canon Doyle's optimism and trust in Lord Ely was misplaced and they were refused their abatement. At a meeting on 20 May 1886, Canon Doyle, in a surprising *volte-face*, suggested the adoption of some of the methods of Fr Davy. He called on the tenants to sign a resolution, which, if anyone broke, they would be boycotted. Fr Hanly, the curate who had been locked out of Davitt Hall, read out the names of the committee and when Andrew Barden's name was called, Peter Connolly, one of Fr Davy's followers, objected to him. Canon Doyle asked the reason for his objection, to which Connolly replied that Barden had broken the combination before and would do so again. Canon Doyle said he thought they had agreed to let bygones be bygones. He called on those tenants who favoured retaining Barden, and 'who favoured unity', to stand on the left while those of the opposite opinion should stand on the right. Nobody moved and Canon Doyle rather arrogantly assumed that to be an acceptance of Barden. The man in question thanked the tenants for electing him and assured them he was unaware he had broken any combination.[21] On 14 August 1886, evictions on the Ely estate took place when 50 men, women and children of 11 families, in Fethard village, were made homeless and on 23 August they marched to New Ross workhouse, in protest, to take up residence there.[22] This was a famous event in the history of the land agitation in Co. Wexford but is outside the scope of this study.

During this second period of activity for Fr Davy, his perspective broadened to encompass other important issues of a wider nationalist and social agenda. He began encouraging the purchase of Irish produce from National League members and promoting cottage industry, specifically in relation to 'bottle-envelopes'. He urged support for it so as to provide a living and some dignity to evicted tenants, thus saving them from being obliged to beg. His social conscience was awakened, in terms of urban poverty, by the appalling living conditions of the poor of Wexford town. He showed a particular sensitivity and understanding of the difficulties facing a working-class woman in bringing her concerns before a middle-class committee, such as theirs.

We see evidence of a sadder and quieter, and perhaps, older and wiser, Fr Davy in the address he delivered at his testimonial to the neighbours and friends among whom he grew to manhood, in which he made use of the adage, 'There's no use crying over spilt milk.'

Behind the scene machinations appear to have taken place before and after his triumphant return to the Hook. Fr Richard Kelly, parish priest of Hook, invited him to act as an adviser to the Ely tenants, at another moment of crisis on the estate, as he had done when he was their curate in 1881–2. The powerful Canon Doyle obviously opposed his involvement and would seem to have been supported by the recently appointed curate in Fr Davy's native Ballymitty, Fr Thomas Meehan. After two visits to the Hook, in February and March 1886, it looks as if he was prevented, by whatever means, from continuing his association with the tenants. The welcome he received on that bleak February day, and the power he could be expected to exercise over the tenants, must have shaken Canon Doyle and made him more determined to prevent 'the troublesome priest's' participation. Fr Davy was rash and unwise to single out one man for chastisement, even if he was being honest. He could have provided better help to the tenants if he had adopted a more subtle approach. However, duplicity was not in his nature and compromise was not a concept he was likely to consider.

After the March 1886 meeting, Fr Davy appears to have effectively dropped out of public life. This was true certainly for the remainder of the 1880s. He must have been sorely grieved by the August evictions on the Ely estate and by his inability to do anything about them. He afterwards served as a curate in Poulpeasty and, eventually, Kiltealy, his last posting. When he died, prematurely, on 28 October 1899, at the age of 55, it was said that he had been in very delicate health for a number of years and was under the medical care of his close friend, Dr Joe Cardiff. He was laid to rest within the walls of the little church at Kiltealy and it was claimed in his obituary, that he was, for many years, the most popular priest in the diocese of Ferns and had stood by Parnell when the split came.[23]

Mary Anne O'Hanlon Walsh, who had come to public attention for a brief period in the early 1880s, married late in life, *c.*1900, a man who was probably her cousin. Andrew Hanlon was between 10 and 20 years her junior, depending on whether one believes the 1901 or 1911 Census. Mary Anne was buried in the family plot in Kilcavan, along with her father, mother and brother, Nicholas. Cantwell deciphers her date of death, from the family tombstone, as 23 May 1932 although there is no reference to her death at that time in the local newspaper.[24]

Nicholas O'Hanlon Walsh continued to be involved in the Irish National League and politics in general for many years. He was elected a poor law rate collector in April 1887 by Wexford board of guardians and continued in that post until his retirement.[25] He regained possession of the family farm in 1898 but never worked it or lived in Knocktartan again.[26] The farm was sold, by Patrick O'Byrne, nephew of Nicholas O'Hanlon Walsh, in 1937, to the Doran family who consolidated both farms and still holds them today.[27] He continued to live at the Land League Cottage, Ballymitty until *c.*1900 when his sister, Mary Anne, married Andrew Hanlon. By 1901, he had moved to live in a boarding house at Common Quay Street, Wexford town. He is listed in both the 1901 and 1911 Censuses as being one of three lodgers of one Johanna Doyle. He was still a poor law rate collector in 1901 but had retired by 1911. Rather intriguingly the 1911 household schedule, in a crossed out entry, reveals that he was a widower who had been married for two years and that two children had been born alive to him but were now deceased. This is the only evidence that he had a wife and family. Neither this anonymous woman, nor Mary Anne's husband, Andrew, appears to have been buried in the family plot. Nicholas died on 16 April 1920 at the boarding house at Common Quay Street. He was 78 years old. According to his obituary, he had fallen in the snow three years previously, which caused him to be confined to his residence. He had become seriously ill a couple of weeks before his death. It was declared that his passing 'marked the end of an epoch in local political life' and that both he and his brother, Fr Davy, had been the prime organizers in south Co. Wexford in the Land League agitation. He was described as 'an Irishman not of the mild type, ardent, determined, advanced in his views'. On Sunday, 18 April 1920, his remains were removed for interment in Kilcavan cemetery.

At the time of Nicholas O'Hanlon Walsh's death the War of Independence was being fought and members of the Irish Volunteers carried his coffin, draped in the Tricolour, from his residence to the hearse. Aldermen of Wexford, about 300 Volunteers, a large Sinn Féin representation and a 'big body' of labourers took part in the procession. The last post was sounded in the Bull Ring. Nearing Ballymitty, the contingent was met by about one hundred local Volunteers and, on arrival at the cemetery, the coffin was shouldered by six of them.[28] In a separate obituary, conscious that Irish independence from Britain had still not been achieved, an unidentified friend wrote: 'In every mind there must have been a feeling of pathos, that he should fall before seeing the victory for which he had laboured during many a dark and hopeless year.'[29] After independence was achieved many streets in Wexford town were renamed in honour of those who had participated in the period 1916–21. Common Quay Street was renamed O'Hanlon Walsh Street.[30]

Conclusion

At the beginning of this work, the community in which the O'Hanlon Walsh family grew up, was examined. Over the 30-year period from 1850 to 1880, the family would have been aware of the drastic fall in population in their parish, through emigration, especially of the poor. Many homes they would have known as children had disappeared, resulting in a more denuded landscape around them, while the comfortable homesteads of their townland remained constant and secure. This continuity was reflected throughout the parish with the larger tenant farmers retaining their holdings. Times may have been difficult for them in the 1850s when their father died and the eldest child, Nicholas, could not have been more than 10 years old. However, Mary Walsh would almost certainly have employed one or two labourers and the neighbours would have helped with harvesting and other chores. In any event, by the late 1860s, things were progressing well for them, with Margaret making an eminently suitable match with a strong farmer from Cushenstown and David, a student for the priesthood, being a recipient of a Roche Foundation bourse at the University of Louvain. They seem to have been unaffected by the Depression of the late 1870s and were described as 'rich' farmers after their eviction.

Many of the larger tenant farmers in the parish seem to have become involved in the Land League agitation at its establishment in late 1880. Clergy from all over the county also played a central role from the beginning. Fr David O'Hanlon Walsh assumed the mantle of leader at its inception and began using his apparent oratorical skills to very good use. The fact that the clergy, generally, appeared to be leading the people, would have made it easier for him, as a priest, to attain that position, but of all the priests of south Wexford in that period, he became the most popular and was surrounded by the most loyal followers. He was certainly seen as a rival by Canon Tom Doyle, particularly after he was appointed to the Hook. This parish was on Canon Doyle's doorstep in Ramsgrange. Canon Doyle was almost 64 years of age when Land League branches began to be established as a result of his initiative in deciding to hold the Wellington Bridge meeting in October 1880. He had been around for a long time and had ministered to the poor of New Ross during the Famine. He was held in great respect by the people and probably resented the young upstart from Ballymitty who was his chief rival for the affections of the people. Canon Doyle saw Fr Davy's methods as extreme and claimed to disapprove of boycotting although he appeared to change his mind on this. Having been in almost total control during the tenure of his curacy in the Hook, Fr Davy lost out to Canon Doyle when he was transferred. When he attempted to become re-involved with the Ely tenants in 1886, Canon Doyle, by whatever means, prevented this from happening. Clergy serving in Bannow parish did not appear to exert such power or control. Fr Boggan, who was curate there during the bitter Poor Law Guardian election campaign of 1884 voted for the nationalist candidate, John McCormack. Fr Patrick Sheridan was parish priest of Bannow throughout the land war but, apart from attending a few meetings, does not appear to have taken a prominent role and did not get involved in the dispute between landlord and tenants on the Boyse estate in Bannow.

The bishop of Ferns, Dr Warren, after an inquiry into his activities, prohibited Fr Davy from preaching or taking an active part in politics. Fr Davy bowed to the letter of his orders if not the spirit. He found other means of continuing his activities, particularly through his faithful followers in the Hook. Dr Browne, successor to Dr Warren, within two months of his consecration, found himself pitted against the people of Hook when he transferred Fr Davy to Castlebridge. It is quite possible that Fr Davy may have suggested the course of action his followers took. In any event, the church door was nailed up for three whole months thus preventing the newly-appointed priest, Fr Lyng, and parishioners from hearing Mass or receiving the sacraments. They eventually gave in but not before Fr Lyng was transferred and another priest appointed. These ordinary, largely uneducated men, were willing to defy the most powerful clergyman in the diocese, albeit in support of another clergyman. What were the religious beliefs of the men who prevented others from entering the church? Presumably, they were baptised Roman Catholics who regularly attended mass and the sacraments, but, in this case, it appears that religious beliefs did not coincide with religious practice.

Any influence that might have been exerted by the absentee marquis of Ely or his agent was well and truly undermined by Fr Davy as soon as he became involved with the tenants. Ely continued to hold some sway with a small minority of tenants, including Andrew Barden, who wished to carry on as normal. Barden ignored the wishes of the Land League and proceeded to use the new facility of the Land Court in order to settle his rent. Conversely, on the Tottenham estate in Knocktartan and adjoining townlands in the parish of Taghmon, the great majority of tenants seemed to abide by the wishes of their landlord, who lived in the next county, and his agent, Thomas Boyd. The interesting voting pattern in the 1884 Poor Law Guardian election would suggest this, with the majority of the Tottenham tenants voting against the nationalist candidate. This would suggest that some landlords, at least, retained considerable influence. Perhaps it helped if they lived closer to their estates than did the marquis of Ely.

What power did government exercise, particularly through its agents in local communities, the Royal Irish Constabulary? The answer would appear to be very little. Despite the Protection Act, although it was deeply resented, people were still carrying on Land League activity and many were proud to be arrested and sent to gaol. Local police constables in the Hook were given a hard time, by both men and women, particularly those who were assigned to keep meetings under surveillance. Even at Taghmon petty sessions, when the Walsh trespass case was being heard, there was uproar in court and a complete disregard for the law. The only person who succeeded in calming the crowd was Fr Davy.

In terms of the factors that cause tensions in a community and, conversely, the factors that make for social cohesion, the Land League could be said to have worked both ways. The land agitation brought people together from all over Co. Wexford and must have given many a great sense of camaraderie. The huge public meetings with their colour and oratory can be expected to have acted as a powerful binding and unifying force among those who attended. On the other hand, it was a major cause of tension between those who supported it and those who disapproved, or did not participate in it. The greatest example of social cohesion in this study is that of the harvesting day on the evicted farm in Knocktartan. Despite the fact that it occurred on a Monday, an ordinary working day, farmers and labourers from all over the parish of Bannow travelled there in convoy to give assistance. In a great show of solidarity, reaping machines lined up to take their turn and the ten acres were harvested in approximately four-and-a-half-hours. However, even on that very special day of neighbours working side-by-side, there was a slight jarring note at the end when Fr Davy made remarks about Taghmon shopkeepers. This was followed by the rather strange announcement in the next edition of the *People*, that, if the people of Taghmon had known for sure that the harvest on the Knocktartan farm was to be saved, they would have been there. This may suggest an undercurrent of tension between shopkeepers and farmers or, perhaps, it may be an earlier manifestation of tensions between tenants on the Tottenham estate. Eleven farmers, from different parts of the parish of Bannow, as well as Nicholas Walsh, waited in line to take their turn at cutting two squares each but none of the 11 names included those of the O'Hanlon Walshs' neighbours who lived on the Knocktartan estate.

Other examples of displays of social cohesion manifested themselves when the prisoners came home from prison and particularly on the day Nicholas O'Hanlon Walsh made his way home to Ballymitty from Fethard-on-Sea. These were instances, at a purely local level, as opposed to the great public meetings, which gathered people together from the towns of Wexford as well as rural parishes throughout the county.

Tensions began to run high in Ballymitty when neighbours of the O'Hanlon Walshs allegedly began to help those who were maintaining their evicted farm for the landlord, Tottenham. This action also gave rise to tensions between farmers and tradesmen, particularly blacksmiths, if they carried out work for these boycotted neighbours. It is possible that the farmers on the Tottenham estate were granted abatements in the wake of the O'Hanlon Walsh eviction in order to ensure there was no further trouble. Surprisingly, there is no evidence of tensions between farmers and labourers, although a dispute arose over the proposed location of labourers' cottages on the Knocktartan estate, which caused further tensions between the O'Hanlon Walshs and their neighbours. This came to a head, pre and post the Poor Law Guardian election in March 1884 when the nationalist candidate was defeated.

Tensions in Hook parish grew more serious and developed into a split between the supporters of Fr Davy and those who opposed him. His chief opponent was Andrew Barden, who had been ostracized by the priest and his followers, and who gave evidence against him to the police and to the bishop.

Interaction between different age groups seems to have been quite healthy and people of varying ages worked together. Profiles of those followers of Fr Davy's, who were arrested and interned, varied in age from seventeen to the late forties. This shows it wasn't only the middle-aged who became involved in the land agitation.

There was considerable mobility, even among the poor, despite the lack of transport. The only modes of transport in the 1880s were on horseback, on various horse or donkey-drawn cars, or on foot. The poor could not afford a horse, some of the luckier ones possessed a donkey and cart, but many had no choice but to resort to walking. People were prepared to walk long distances as is evidenced by the walk, on Nicholas O'Hanlon Walsh's return to Ballymitty from Fethard-on-Sea, which took four-and-a-half hours to complete. People did not always marry within their own locality as is evidenced by Margaret Walsh's marriage to Patrick O'Byrne of Cushenstown. Cushenstown was at least 12 miles from Knocktartan and it would be of interest to know how they met. The popularity of the fife and drum bands also led to interaction and exchanges between parishes. The bands were a source of social cohesion and lacked the later competitive, and sometimes confrontational, rivalry of parish GAA teams.

Urban and rural inhabitants would have met at the public meetings and conventions, many of which were held in the towns of Wexford and New Ross. Fr Davy became involved in urban affairs when he served as a curate in Wexford and urged the rural population to make their purchases in nationalist shops in the town.

Women played an important role in the communities of the Hook and Bannow at this time. The meeting of the Ladies' Land League in Hook on 12 December 1881 was a prime example of their commitment to the land agitation and their freedom to spend most of Sunday at a meeting. Women and girls of varying ages were in attendance. Mary Anne Walsh, sister of Fr Davy and Nicholas, stepped into the breach when one brother was silenced and the other in prison, and provided continuity of agitation on the Ely estate and the adjoining estates of Dunbrody and Tintern. It is salutary to note that, at a later meeting, she called for the emulation of Anna Parnell, rather than Charles Stewart. Indeed, she and the women of both Bannow and Hook Ladies' Land Leagues were shown greater appreciation from the men of the parishes than Anna Parnell received from her brother. Both Dr Joe Cardiff and the Revd Patrick Doyle showered praise on the heads of the women for their work. Dr Cardiff, proving he was a man of advanced views, looked forward to the day when they would speak in public. Women appeared on public platforms and were even, sometimes, named in the *People*. They were not all middle-class women either. The police correspondence informs us that members of the Hook Ladies' League came from the ranks of the small farmers and labourers.

Fr Davy understood the power of imagery as much as the power of oratory. He used visual aids, in terms of placards and posters, and images, with the idea that they would be imprinted on minds. An important image was created by his entrances into villages on horseback, where the majority of people gathered would be on foot and did not own a horse. He, as their leader, would be in an elevated position above the crowd. He appreciated the implicit sense of ownership achieved by the act of naming. He renamed houses, streets and townlands. Above all, he renamed his own family, which was certainly unusual, and perhaps even unique, among tenant farmers in Co. Wexford in the nineteenth century. It may be that he wanted to impress upon their landlord, Tottenham, that their pedigree was older and better than his. Holders of the Irish and Norman names of O'Hanlon Walsh had a better right to the soil of Ireland than one with the New English name of Tottenham. Fr Davy also used dramatic effects, assuming the persona of Dr Joe Cardiff, for one afternoon after his arrest, by wearing his apparel and driving into New Ross in his croydon. It is a safe bet that everybody in the town would remember the day Dr Cardiff was arrested and imprisoned. His behaviour is reminiscent of a modern day politician trying to grab the attention of the media. He encouraged the singing of songs about the Land League, land-grabbers and such famous ones as 'The Wearing of the Green' and 'The Harp without the Crown' in order to encourage the people and to raise their spirits. His careful selection of a platform in the ruins of a cottage on the harvesting day was, again, intended to portray a powerful image of the evicted family 'without a roof'.

Despite all the tensions and alleged intimidation, especially in the Hook, and the huge public meetings, there was almost a complete lack of violence in the two communities. The only 'agrarian outrage' that occurred in this period was the breaking of the windows in the gatelodge of Loftus Hall. The claims of incitement to murder could not be taken too seriously, although one cannot deny that they would be somewhat intimidating. They would appear to have been more in the realm of idle threats.

In all of these public gatherings there is little evidence of drunkenness, although one must bear in mind that the *People* might not have reported this type of anti-social behaviour among followers of the Land League. The only reports available are two extracts from the *Daily Express*, one contained in the police correspondence. One was no more than suspicions that Fr Davy may have been drunk when he drove into New Ross in Dr Cardiff's apparel and made straight for Ryan's public house. The other instance was a report in the same newspaper, which was quoted by Fr Davy at the meeting in Taghmon on 15 August 1881. This extract claimed that the 'Hook 200' had been 'well-primed with whiskey' when they arrived at the scene of the Knocktartan eviction, a claim that was utterly refuted by Fr Davy.

Symbols of popular culture favoured by the people, along with the ballads and the fife and drum bands, were flags, banners and greenery, which were used for decorative purposes at all meetings and celebrations. Arches across the roads displaying various mottoes were popular, and representations of Erin, as a young and beautiful woman, clad in a green gown, were characteristic of the Parnellite era.

What was the legacy of the O'Hanlon Walsh family? From the viewpoint of its own economic situation, the answer has to be glorious failure. It is difficult to find examples, in Co. Wexford, of other families allowing themselves to be evicted for a principle, certainly in the early 1880s. This may have happened on the Tottenham estate at Ballykerogue and Dunganstown in 1887. However, in 1881, the O'Hanlon Walshs stood alone. Fr Davy's methods may have been extreme but, if the agitation was to succeed, unity had to be ensured. Even Canon Doyle, when he was faced with no alternative, felt the need to adopt some of his methods. Fr Davy certainly had the power to lift the spirits of all who heard him if the reports of 'storms of applause', cheering and waving of handkerchiefs, can be believed.

Mary Anne O'Hanlon Walsh made a brief, but possibly significant, contribution to the cause of women's role in public life. She appeared to be the only woman of her time in Co. Wexford whose speeches at Ladies' Land League meetings were sometimes published in the *People*. Nicholas O'Hanlon Walsh continued, doggedly, with his involvement in politics, in his own quiet way, throughout the 1880s and thereafter. His continued participation is outside the scope of this study. However, as a link had been established between the Land League and the rebellion of 1798 in a Knocktartan cornfield, so a link was established between the Land League, in the person of Nicholas O'Hanlon Walsh, and the War of Independence. When he died in 1920 his coffin was draped in the Tricolour and carried to its place of rest by Volunteers from Ballymitty.

Notes

ABBREVIATIONS

AI National Archives of Ireland   RIC Royal Irish Constabulary
LI National Library of Ireland   UCD University College Dublin
S Ordnance Survey of Ireland

INTRODUCTION

Thomas Butler, *A parish and its people* (Wellington Bridge, 1984), p. 29.

T. Jones Hughes, 'Continuity and change in rural County Wexford in the nineteenth century' in K. Whelan and W. Nolan (eds.), *Wexford: history and society* (Dublin, 1987), pp 362–64.

I. FAMILY BACKGROUND

Valuation office, Perambulation Books of Griffith's valuation, County of Wexford, parish of Ballymitty, townland of Knocktartan, Oct. 1852.

2 *People* (Wexford), 20 Apr. 1920.

John V. Gahan, *The secular priests of the diocese of Ferns* (Strasbourg, 2000), pp 19–20.

N.A.I., Census of Ireland, 1911, Household Schedules, parish of Ballymitty, townland of Ballymitty.

5 Ibid., 1901.

6 Ibid., parish of Carnagh, townland of Cushenstown.

7 Valuation office, Perambulation books of Griffith's valuation, 1852.

8 Maynooth College archives, Belgian bourses, 114/9.

9 Gahan, *Secular priests*, pp 19–20.

10 Maynooth College archives, Belgian bourses, 113/4/24.

11 Ibid., 113/4/21, translation by W.H. Grattan-Flood.

12 N.A.I., Census of Ireland, 1901, County Wexford 77/2, Form N.

13 Gahan, *Secular priests,* p. 219.

14 *People* (Wexford), 20 Apr. 1920.

15 Valuation office, Cancellation Books, 1920.

16 Gahan, *Secular priests*, p. 20

17 Ibid., 20 Oct. 1880.

18 Séamus S. de Vál, 'Father Tom, the Land League priest' in *The Past*, 12 (1978), pp 23–30.

19 *People* (Wexford), 27 Oct. 1880.

20 Ibid., 23 Feb. 1881.

21 Ibid., 13 Nov. 1880.

22 Ibid., 23 Feb. 1881.

23 Ibid.

24 Ibid., 5 Mar. 1881.

25 Ibid., 12 Mar. 1881.

26 Ibid., 26 Mar. 1881.

27 Ibid., 2 Apr. 1881.

28 Ibid., 20 Apr. 1881.

29 *Landowners in Ireland: owners of one acre and upwards 1876* (Dublin, 1876).

30 T. Dooley, *Sources for the history of landed estates in Ireland* (Dublin, 2000), p. 8.

31 *Landowners in Ireland* (Dublin, 1876).

32 *People* (Wexford), 2 July 1881.

33 Dooley, *Sources*, p. 10.

34 *People* (Wexford), 11 Aug. 1880.

35 NAI, CSO ICR, Return of outrages 1879–93,

36 NAI, Crown Book at Assizes, Co. Kilkenny, spring 1863 – spring 1885.

37 *People* (Wexford), 26 Mar. 1881.

38 Ibid., 2 July 1881.

39 NAI, CSO RP 26992/1881, Taghmon meeting.

40 NAI, CSO RP 188/1882, Cases to be taken under Protection of Person and Property Act, 29 Dec. 1881.

41 *People* Wexford, 17 Aug. 1881.

42 NAI, CSO RP 188/1882), Inquiry into Fr. Walsh, 22 Dec. 1881,

43 NAI, CSO RP 188/1882, Cases to be taken under Protection Act, 29 Dec. 1881

44 Thomas Butler, *A parish and its people* (Wellington Bridge, 1984), pp 129–30.

45 *People* (Wexford), 31 Aug. 1881.

46 NAI, CSO RP 188/1882, Constable Allshire to Sub-Inspector Wilson, 22 Nov. 1881,

47 *People* (Wexford), 19 Oct. 1881.

2. THE REVD DAVID O'HANLON WALSH

1 NAI, CSO RP 188/1882, Inquiry into Fr Walsh, 22 Dec. 1881.

2 *People* (Wexford), 5 and 26 Mar. 1881.

3 Ibid., 16 Apr. 1881.

4 Ibid., 21 May 1881.

5 NAI, CSO RP 188/1882, Ball to Inspector General, 1 Oct. 1881.

6 Ibid., 8 Oct. 1881.

7 *People* (Wexford), 19 Oct. 1881.

8 Gahan, *Secular priests*, p. 307.

9 NAI, CSO RP 188/1882), Mullan to Ball and Ball to Inspector General, 25 Oct. 1881.

10 44 & 45 Victoria, c.4.

11 Ibid.

12   NAI CSO RP 188/1882, Palmer to Inspector General, 30 Oct. 1881.

13   Ibid., Wilson to McMahon and McMahon to Under Secretary, 8 Nov. 1881.

14   Ibid., Allshire to Inspector General, 2 Nov. 1881.

15   Ibid., Taylor to Chief Secretary Forster, 10 Nov. 1881.

16   Ibid., Ball to Inspector General, 20 Nov. 1881.

17   Ibid., Palmer to Jones, 30 Nov. 1881.

18   Ibid., Taylor to Chief Secretary, 3 Dec. 1881.

19   Ibid., Ball to Jones, 14 Dec. 1881.

20   *People* (Wexford), 31 Aug. 1881.

21   NAI, CSO RP 188/1882, Inquiry into Fr. Walsh, 22 Dec. 1881.

22   Ibid., Boland to Ball, 29 Dec. 1881.

23   *People* (Wexford), 16 Jan. 1882.

3. IMPRISONMENT AND EVICTIONS

1   NAI, CSO RP 188/1882, Robert Kennedy to Burke, Under Secretary, 22 Jan. 1882.

2   *People* (Wexford), 1 Mar. 1882.

3   Ibid., 4 Mar. 1882.

4   Ibid., 8 Mar. 1882.

5   NAI, CSO RP 188/1882, Godfrey Taylor to Chief Secretary Forster, 23 Mar. 1882.

6   *People* (Wexford), 15 Feb. 1882.

7   Ibid., 15 Mar. 1882.

8   Ibid., 28 Mar. 1882.

9   Ibid., 15 Apr. 1882.

10   NAI, CSO RP 188/1882, Fitzgerald to inspector general, 18 Apr. 1882.

11   *People* (Wexford), 26 Apr. 1882.

12   Ibid., 21 June, 1882.

13   Valuation office, Cancellation Books, townland of Ballymitty.

14   *People* (Wexford), 12 July 1882.

15   NAI, CSO RP 188/1882, Notice from marquis of Ely to tenants, 8 May 1882.

16   Ibid., Robert Kennedy to Under Secretary Burke, 16 Sept. 1882,

17   *People* (Wexford), 27 Sept. 1882.

18   Ibid., 30 Sept. 1882.

19   Ibid., 28 Oct. 1882.

4. TENSIONS IN TWO COMMUNITIES

1   *People* (Wexford), 28 Oct. 1882.

2   Ibid., 7 Mar. 1883.

3   Ibid., 4 Apr. 1883.

4   Ibid., 13 Jan. 1883.

5   Ibid.. 17 Feb. 1883.

6   Ibid. 12 June 1883.

7   Ibid. 8 Sept. 1883.

8   Ibid. 13 Oct. 1883.

9   Ibid., 5 Jan. 1884.

10   Ibid., 31 Oct. 1883.

11   Ibid., 7 Nov. 1883.

12   Valuation Office, Cancellation Books, townland of Ardinagh Great.

13   *People* (Wexford), 24 Nov. 1883.

14   Ibid., 8 Dec. 1883.

15   Ibid., 9 Feb. 1884.

16   Valuation Office, Cancellation Books, townlands of Knocktartan and Ballymitty.

17   *People* (Wexford), 16 Feb. 1884.

18   Dept. of Folklore, UCD: Schools collection, Ballymitty School, 1935.

19   Ibid. 26 Mar. 1884.

20   Gahan, *Secular priests*, p. 404.

21   *People* (Wexford), 19 Apr. 1884.

22   Gahan, *Secular priests*, pp 405, 19–20.

23   *People* (Wexford), 13 Apr. and 27 Apr. 1889.

24   Interview with Mr Tom Hickey, Ramstown, Fethard-on-Sea, 7 June 2001.

25   Gahan, *Secular priests*, p. 110.

26   *People* (Wexford), 22 November 1884.

5. THE REVD DAVID O'HANLON WALSH IN WEXFORD TOWN

1   *People* (Wexford), 2 August 1884.

2   Ibid., 6 Aug. 1884.

3   Ibid., 28 Mar. 1885.

4   Ibid., 27 May 1885.

5   Ibid., 20 June and 11 July 18?

6   Ibid., 16 Sept. 1885.

7   Ibid., 19 Sept. 1885.

8   Ibid., 26 Sept. and 7 Oct. 1885.

9   Ibid., 7 Oct. 1885.

10   Ibid., 2 Dec. 1885.

11   Ibid., 16 Dec. 1885.

12   Ibid., 13 Jan. 1886.

13   Ibid., 10 Feb. 1886.

14   Ibid., 13 Feb. 1886.

15   Ibid., 12 Apr. 1885.

16   Ibid., 24 Feb. 1886.

17   Ibid., 10 Feb. 1886.

18   Gahan, *Secular priests*, p. 352.

19   *People* (Wexford), 13 Mar. 1886.

20   Ibid., 5 May 1886.

21   Ibid., 2 June 1886.

22   Ibid., 2 Sept., 1886.

23   Ibid., 1 Nov., 1899.

24   Brian Cantwell, *Memorials the Dead*, *vii*, *South-East Wexf?* (1984), p.53.

25   Richard Roche, 'Forth and Bargy – a place apart' in K. Whelan and W. Nolan (eds.), *Wexford: history and society* (Dublin, 1987), p. 119.

26   Valuation office, Cancellation Books, townland of Knocktartan.

27   Ibid.

28   *People* (Wexford), 21 Apr. 1920.

29   Ibid., 24 Apr. 1920.

30   Conversation with Jarlath Glynn, Wexford library on 12 Nov. 2001.